A N
E N C Y C L O P E D I A
O F
TABLES

AN
ENCYCLOPEDIA
OF
TABLES

SIMON YATES

Grange
BOOKS

A QUANTUM BOOK

Published by Grange Books
an imprint of Grange Books Plc
The Grange
Kingsnorth Industrial Estate
Hoo, nr. Rochester
Kent ME3 9ND

Copyright © 1989 Quintet Publishing ltd

This edition printed 1999

ISBN 1-85627-872-7

QUMEOT

This book is produced by
Quantum Books Ltd
6 Blundell Street
London N7 9BH

Printed and bound in Singapore by
Star Standard Industries (PTE) Ltd

CONTENTS

INTRODUCTION

This early 20th-century view of the Meyer May house (designed by Frank Lloyd Wright) shows Wright's individuality combined with European trends. The surfaces, whether of the walls or of the furniture, tend to be flat and rectangular. The influence of the Scottish architect and designer Charles Rennie Mackintosh appears in the geometric balustrade and the almost medieval weight of the lamp columns, but the novelty of the umbrella stand in the hall table shows an original mind.

One of the interests in collecting antique furniture surely lies in the history that has developed alongside the evolving styles and decorative motifs. Each piece has an individual design background, reflecting both artistic and social trends fashionable at the time of its construction. In this book, a selection of tables is used to illustrate the development of the Western table over the ages, concentrating on examples from the 17th century onwards. Function and traditional use and the craftsmanship, techniques and materials used in the making are all relevant to the way shape and design have changed and developed over the years.

During the 16th and 17th centuries, the use of tables became increasingly specific, reflecting the needs and status of the owner. The travelling life of much of the medieval nobility, and the poverty of most of the population, meant that little more was needed than the multi-purpose medieval bench, used variously for seating, sleeping and storage, as well as a table. By the end of the 16th century, however, the European division between fashionable ornate tables found at court and the unchanging rough-hewn practical table of most of the populace was created and widened rapidly. It is the furniture of the fashionable that has lasted, coming from a more sheltered environment, and which is of most interest to us now. It was the aristocracy who commissioned the finest cabinetmakers and designers to create tables for their homes, and it was the wealthy that were keenest to keep up with the latest designs – a trend which continues today.

Soon after the beginnings of refinement in decoration at the time of the Italian Renaissance, separate table styles for separate functions began to emerge. Tables designed for writing were first found in Italy in the luxurious 16th-century palaces of Florence and Rome; dining tables developed away from the simple trestle and board; and the ornate courts of Louis XIV and XV saw the flowering of a myriad of small tables and desks – the writing table, the *table de nuit*, the dressing table, the occasional table, and after the introduction of tea from the Orient, the tea table.

The fact that tables were required for each of these separate functions gives the 20th-century observer a good idea of contemporary social developments. The influence of the Oriental trade routes – through the import of tea, but more importantly through the import of woods, materials and exquisite artworks – had a lasting impact on Europe, both artistically and socially. Delicate, round, candle-holding guéridons, first seen in the 16th century, were named after young black pages used mainly to hold lighting at the European courts, and are a reminder of the enormous wealth and status that growing trade through the Colonies brought to so many aristocrats and merchants – some of which was presumably spent on commissioning tables to decorate their splendid homes. The Georgian obsession with draughtsmanship, architecture and landscaping is reflected in their intricate gadgetted tables.

But although function is an obvious way to classify tables, the materials used and decorative styles employed are just as important. Generally made of wood, the very earliest tables from Ancient Egypt, Greece and Rome have rarely survived. Although the Egyptians prized ebony for its hardness and colour, the Romans probably used mainly light woods, such as pine and beech, which are easily destroyed by insects, damp and wear. In Europe, the native woods of oak and walnut were dense and

durable, but even so, few European tables from before the 1500s have lasted to today. The European tradition of carving, however, was developed during the Renaissance, as woods such as walnut were easily sculpted, and this art was readily adapted to the new, harder woods imported to Europe after the explorations of the 15th and 16th centuries. Ebony and the exotic zebra and rosewoods were ideal for the decorative art of veneer, a technique which uses thin strips of wood to create stunning patterns and designs, and which was to change the face – and structure – of furniture from the 16th century onwards. The designs of Chippendale in the 18th century made the best possible use of mahogany, showing its fine grain and deep colour to best effect.

In the 19th century, industrialization and newly-discovered techniques of metalworking saw a proliferation of table styles, both structural and decorative. The Great Exhibition of 1851, held at London's Crystal Palace, was a showcase for imaginative – although sometimes excessive – furniture design, with tables made of cast iron, bent wood and papier mâché, amongst many others. Over the last century, synthetic materials have opened the door to another range of design possibilities, with aluminium and plywood preceding glass and plastic.

Tables, with their flat surfaces and straight lines, are open to an endless variety of ornament, and consistently reflect the changing tastes of their times. Craftsmen and designers have drawn from sources as diverse as religion, archeology and nature in their search for inspiration, and the different design styles over the last few hundred years – Gothic, Baroque, Rococo, Classical – clearly indicate the breadth of influence. In some cases, the decorative function of a table is without a doubt more important than its practical use: the gilded 17th-century console table was originally designed to fill an unseemly gap on the walls of the Mirror Gallery in Louis XIV's Château de Versailles; the virtuoso marble-topped tables of the Italian 18th century were primarily made for display. Decorated Regency breakfast tables combine display and function, tilting down during the day when not in use, thus making the top fully visible.

When trying to unravel the different strands of design which influence any one piece, classification can often be more of a hindrance than a help. European furniture design periods have generally been named after monarchies (Louis XIV, Queen Anne), architecture (Gothic, Classical), governments (Empire) or craftsmen (Chippendale, Sheraton, Hepplewhite); each of these can be further qualified by a country of origin, and will not necessarily refer to the same time span. American Queen Anne, for example, was produced in the United States some 50 years after the end of the reign of the English Queen in 1714 – its restrained elegance was very popular with the settlers. Many of these styles were revived at a later date, and either imitated with a contemporary feel (such as with Victorian Rococo) or reproduced using materials and construction techniques preferred by later craftsmen. Nonetheless, some form of descriptive classification is required, and if treated with caution can be very helpful in identifying the underlying influences on a piece.

The examples in this book have been divided into chapters covering each century, and arranged in chronological order. This is not to suggest an abrupt change in style at the end of each century, however; furniture styles have always evolved gradually, as have the societies they were made to serve.

BEFORE

1600

The Winter Parlour (c1582) from the Swiss Castle of Wiggen shows the range of 16th-century styles available in Europe. The trestle table is Gothic, the chair backs are carved with Renaissance scrolls and shells, and the door is framed by revived Classical columns. The overall effect is slightly busy and confused, lacking the clarity of 18th-century Classical revival which is clear and cool. It is an excellent use of pine giving a homely but interesting result.

In the pre-Christian world, furniture was scarce except in the homes of the very wealthy. Nonetheless, when Tutankhamun was buried 14 centuries before Christ with much of his furniture (for use in the after life), it is curious that there was little like a formal table. It is possible that some of the stools might have served the same purpose; wall paintings and vases dating from the time of the Greeks and Romans clearly show small tables resembling stools being used for eating and gambling. On the whole, these give the appearance of being very plain (although there are rare illustrations of the top surfaces), but more elaborate examples in marble have survived.

There is plenty of evidence that tables were in use in many other parts of the world, including Syria (tables are often mentioned in the Bible) and Western Asia. In China, tables were used well before the 1st century AD, and chairs and tables were employed ceremonially and domestically by the 10th century. In Europe, a brass stand from c. BC100 was found at Pompeii, Italy, cast and chased elaborately in bronze, its three animal legs topped with sphinxes and joined by curving stretchers. Although it is not certain that it was a table, it resembles closely the form developed by the time of Christ and the Roman Empire a century later. A Romano-German sarcophagus from cAD300 is decorated with a carved three-legged table with a half-round top and, again, animal legs and feet, and by AD400 free standing, wall and cross-framed tables were all in existence.

Little is known of European furniture between AD500 and AD1,000. To trace its development through this period, we have to rely on evidence from paintings and other artworks. Illustrated manuscripts from c1100 show monks and saints seated and writing on chair rests, but rarely using tables of any sort. The likelihood is that most were of rough construction, with thickly sawn planks for the top, and four legs. Tables were not used for storage, as now, and were therefore less necessary than other pieces of furniture – possessions would have been stored elsewhere, in chests, coffers or in built-in cupboards. In the Middle Ages, the bench served many functions – as a bed, a seat, and almost certainly as a table – and it was possibly with the accumulation of wealth and a more settled lifestyle that permanent pieces of furniture began to take root.

More examples have survived from after 1400 or so, however, although tables from well into the 16th century remain difficult to find. The plainness of the medieval table, often covered with cloths or table-carpets, was gradually embellished with the Renaissance vogue for ornament, first seen in Italy in the 15th century. These Renaissance examples were different in that the basic forms were decorated with abundant Classical motifs, among them swags, urns and grotesque masks, drawn from Ancient Greek and Roman art and architecture. (Whether directly or indirectly, Classicism has always played a major part in Western furniture decoration and even continues to influence design of the present day.)

Renaissance Italy was a great trading nation, which exposed its designers to a variety of foreign influences: Venice's links with the Far East encouraged a taste for chinoiserie and the inlay of both exotic woods and ivory, and the city's proximity to the Arabic world resulted in the adoption of arabesque patterns. Such abstract motifs are widely used and have been perfected by Muslims, because their faith forbids the use of human and animal imagery.

As the Renaissance took hold throughout Europe, these same motifs are found on tables in France, Germany, the Netherlands and in England. Elizabethan 16th-century refectory tables no longer stood on simple trestles, but might well have sported bulbous, carved legs. Stretchers, added originally for strength, became an integral part of a table, providing additional surfaces for the favoured carved-wood decoration. Northern European nations were still influenced by the heavier Gothic style, but the influential pattern books by Han Vredeman de Vries, published in Holland c1580, showed tables employing a typically rectangular style evolved from a combination of Gothic and Rococo.

While still scarce in the majority of homes, the 1500s witnessed a flowering of furniture in the Renaissance spirit, commissioned by the royalty and aristocracy of Europe. Fontainebleau Palace (built and furnished by France's François I, 1515–47) contained some beautiful decorated tables, as did Henry VIII's Hampton Court in England. The gap rapidly widened between court furniture for the wealthy who demanded the latest styles, and the rough, practical all-purpose table for the poorer population, which remained virtually unchanged as the centuries passed.

PRE-1600

1. A Gothic Oak Coffer, c1500

Although some of the richer residences of this date might have had separate tables, in the majority of houses the coffer was used as a general piece of furniture serving as storage space, bench, table and even bed. The distinction between coffers and chests was minimal, although generally a chest travelled and a coffer did not. A coffer could be as large as 12ft (3.65m) long and 4ft (1.2m) wide. In 1438, the Company of Coffee Makers asked Richard III to prohibit the import of Flemish furniture in order to protect their home market.

This English example is set off the ground (to keep it away from damp and insects), and has a simple hinged top. The planks are joined with tongue-and-groove timber, and the front shows typical deep-carved 'tracery' decoration (so-named after the patterned windows of churches and cathedrals).

2. A French Henri II Walnut Centre Table, c1580

As in the rest of Europe, France produced little furniture of note before 1400. The few chairs, stools and tables that did exist were largely plain and Gothic in style, made of thick planks and joined with pegs. This changed with the Renaissance, which spread from Italy throughout Europe during the 15th century, revolutionizing all branches of art. During the reign of François I (1515–47), the prevailing decorative style in France changed from Gothic to Italian-influenced Renaissance designs; the showpiece of the new style was the Chateau de Fontainebleau outside Paris. This was the centre for the school of Fontainebleau, greatly influenced by the Italian, Francesco Primaticcio (1505–70), and responsible for introducing Italian designs in furniture production. These included carved motifs and table friezes, which were decorated with designs such as slender naked nymphs, chubby angels with garlands of flowers, satyr masks, strapwork and scrolls.

By the time Henri II (1547–59) succeeded François I, the applied arts in France were in turmoil. Apart from the highly decorated pieces displayed at Fontainebleau, another style, geometric and simple, was emerging in reaction to Renaissance excess.

This table belongs to the simpler French style, which stressed the architectural elements of the Renaissance movement. Based on an overall geometric plan, the legs, shaped like columns, are distinctly non-Gothic. Although there is a small amount of turned ornament, there is very little carving.

3. An Oak Court Cupboard, c1600

This early type of sideboard takes its name from the French word, *court*, meaning short. English-made, cupboards such as this are first mentioned in documents from the reign of Elizabeth I (1559–1603), and in Shakespeare's *Romeo and Juliet* servants are told to 'remove the court cupboard and look to the plate' – meaning to clear the furniture and utensils after eating so as to leave space for dancing. The drawer in the frieze probably would have been used to store linen or valuables, and the top would have displayed food and plate.

The traditional English court cupboard usually had three tiers – here, for example, there may well have been another tier on top of the two remaining, but furniture was constantly altered and adapted. The drawer is decorated with 'stop fluting', and the front legs are bulbous compared to the flatter back legs. The cupboard is solidly built, with mortice-and-tenon joints throughout pegged with wood – the pegs can clearly be seen on the bottom rail.

4. A Spanish Walnut Table, c1600

This table is typical of many produced in Spain during the 17th century, and may well date from very early in the 1600s. Plain, with elegant bobbin-turned legs, it has the S-shaped iron stretchers that were found on a great deal of Mediterranean furniture of this period. Iron stretchers are elegant and stronger than wood, as well as pliable, so it is perhaps surprising that they were not adopted elsewhere in Europe before the 19th century. The tops of these tables were often attached to their trestle legs by a loose mortice-and-tenon joint. This allowed the whole table to fold when the stretchers were removed.

There is a noticeable lack of carved or other decoration here, although it was not due to a lack of skill. Spain and Portugal were at the peak of their power in the mid 16th century, and many finely carved and inlaid cabinets date from both the 1500s and 1600s. A more likely reason is that the table would have been covered with an embroidered tablecloth or table-carpet showing mythological, biblical or folklore scenes, and would therefore require less embellishment. This was a continuation of a custom common all over Europe, as can be seen from the very fine 'table-carpets' in the Victoria & Albert Museum, London, which date from the late medieval period onward.

1600
TO
1700

Easy Come, Easy Go
*When Jan Steen painted this Dutch interior in 1661
he was illustrating a proverb and perhaps
disapproving of the gamblers' winnings being
frittered away on wine and food. It also shows a
page from the history of furniture in Puritan
Holland; Puritanism was also prevalent in England
and America around this time.
The table is fairly plain, the thick top resting on
supports relieved by a little gilt and carving. It does,
however, show some influence from extravagant
styles popular in France and Italy. A carpet and a
linen cloth have both been partly rolled back for
dining.*

At the onset of the 17th century, there emerged three main types of everyday table in the homes of the wealthy. A large communal dining table was used in the great hall of a stately home (this could seat up to 50 diners); a smaller, private table, made of thick timbers and often of oak, for writing or dining; and the folding table, its flap supported by the relatively sophisticated gate leg and requiring hinges. As the century progressed, and homes generally became smaller, tables which could be extended for occasional use became popular. Although formal public life for royalty took place in massive chambers – as epitomized by Louis XIV's Château de Versailles – smaller private apartments and informal chambers required a different style of furnishings.

The Château de Versailles, built during the reign of Louis XIV (1643–1715), became the standard for European taste. The showpiece of the Sun King was filled with furniture which included tables as extravagant in their size and colour as the palace they occupied (the creation of such court furniture often fell within the domain of the architect). The 'weight' of these pieces strongly impressed itself on a room, and furniture form became an integral part of interior design. A heightened overall effect was achieved by the use of the innovative console table in particular, which stood against a wall, often surmounted by a mirror forming a pattern with the now larger vertical windows. Large palaces needed private apartments, and for these too smaller tables were made, some compact enough for the bedside, and including drawers to hold cosmetics and writing materials. Likewise, the ritual of dining became more complex, and so side and serving tables were devised, as were wine tables and games tables.

In England, the move towards extravagant European fashions was halted by the execution of the king, Charles I (ruled 1626–1649), and the establishment of a Puritan state under Oliver Cromwell. Tables reverted back to being plain, uncarved and functional. But with the Restoration of the monarchy in the 1660s came an influx of continental practices.

Tea was introduced from the Orient during the 17th century, and the ritual for taking tea became part of the aristocratic social life. Ham House, outside London, the residence of the Countess Lauderdale, was fully refurbished in prevailing European styles in the 1670s. An inventory dating from 1679 suggests that tea parties were already well established, listing an 'Indian furnace for tee garnished wt silver'. And as well as tea tables, there were card tables, tables for lighting and occasional tables that were unfolded when necessary.

English tables began to sport carving and gilding, these handsome embellishments often executed by Hugenot craftsmen such as Daniel Marot and the French carving family, the Pelletiers. These were religious refugees, who had left their native France after the revocation of the Edict of Nantes by Louis XIV in 1685, ending nearly a century of religious freedom and causing many protestants to leave the country. Many moved to Holland, and thence to England when the protestant William of Orange succeeded to the throne of catholic James II.

The move towards flamboyant decoration, and structure based on beauty, not support or function, came once more from Italian sources, and the naturalistic forms of the Baroque fashion. Italy dominated European taste with its Baroque furniture design, perpetuating the Renaissance love of decoration. At its best, it created colourful and dramatic tables on sweeping, scrolling gilt supports; at worst, it produced heavy clumsy tables with little functional value. Italian tables tended to be of soft wood, sometimes poorly carved, although there are some finely carved examples by the sculptor Antonio Corradini in Venice.

France had already established its own style influenced by the Baroque affection for colour and the exotic. The decorative art of veneering, originally known to the ancient civilizations of Egypt, Greece and Rome, allowed highly-skilled craftsmen to make full use of the finely figured hardwoods which arrived with the opening of world trade routes. The French term *ébéniste* (cabinetmaker) refers to the preference of early veneerers for ebony. Veneers were adapted for marquetry and parquetry (naturalistic or geometric designs respectively), and cabinet makers were keen to exploit the decorative possibilities of wood grains and other materials. The great cabinetmaker and favourite of Louis XV, André-Charles Boulle (1842–1732) was renowned for both his furniture designs and for his intricate tortoiseshell and brass inlay work, which made the most of colour and texture.

By 1700, tables of bright red patterned marble on carved-wood bases of shells, figures and foliage were no more surprising than examples featuring Boulle inlay, or constructions of solid silver. Among the factors leading to such ostentation were the increase in new wealth and a sheer love of show. There is no doubt that, compared to their medieval counterparts, tables had come of age, in terms of both design and decoration.

5. An English James I Oak Dining Table, *c*1620

In the medieval period, dining halls consisted of a 'high', or 'top', table raised on a platform. At this table, which held the salt, sat the most important diners; the rest of the eaters sat at other tables, 'below the salt'. During the transition from this tradition to a single large table, as seen here, trestle tables which could be folded away were used – Penshurst Place in Kent, England, contains three famous oak trestle tables from the late 15th century.

By 1580, however, joined tables had arrived. They generally had a fixed top, six legs and stretchers between the feet, used as both foot rests and to stack away the benches or stools which were sat on. In the late 16th century, these tables were often heavily carved with elaborate frieze decorations, but by 1600 they were plainer and more stylized.

This example is fairly typical, with a little turning on the legs, some carving on the frieze where the rails meet the legs, and mortice-and-tenon pegged joints throughout. By the end of the century, the realization that these tables were too large led to the development of extending flaps. Tables such as these were also used to play 'shovel board' in Tudor times, a game closely related to 'shove halfpenny', wherein coins are pushed along a flat surface with the palm of the hand.

6. An Oak Folding Table, *c*1620

This table uses the simplest of mechanisms to open out. The top is opened like the lid of a box, with wrought-iron hinges fixed with nails, and the back leg swings out as a support, ie 'gate leg'. It has standard features for its time, including hexagonal shape, plain but slightly tapered legs and a drawer in the flat, stylized frieze.

Tables such as this appeared in almost all inventories of the big houses of the period. For example, the 1641 inventory of Tart Hall noted 'an ovall Table of wanscote with falling sides'. 'Wanscote', or 'wainscot', is derived from the word 'wain', or wagon. During the 15th century, wainscot came to mean 'wagon wood' (ie a wagon load of wood or timber); hence its use to refer to any wood for furniture or panelling.

7

8

7. A 17th-Century Folding Table, c1630

This folding table makes use of two gate legs, one on each side. The double gate leg was generally employed where the table was larger, as here, and so needed more support. By 1670, tables seating as many as 10 were made, with two gate legs on each side to accommodate extending flaps. Another popular variation allowed the table to fold away altogether. This utilized gate legs which pivoted, and a top that tilted in the manner of 18th-century breakfast tables.

This fairly basic example shows many standard features of James I and Charles I styles. The legs are solid and only very slightly turned, but the decoration is more pronounced; there is strapwork on the lower stretcher, and a running frieze of scrolling just below the top. Mortice-and-tenon joints secured by pegs can be seen on the inside of the legs.

8. A Spanish Table of Refectory Type, c1650

This refectory-style table was the alternative to the Spanish trestle table. It is of heavier build, with a large, overhanging top, and a deep frieze with two drawers. The table's stout baluster-turned columns are joined by a substantial H-shaped stretcher; pieces of similar design were also made in France during the early 17th century.

Much of the decoration shows Moorish influence. The southern third of Spain, which included Granada and Seville, was occupied by the Moors and their Islamic culture until the fall of Granada in 1492. The decorated panels on the frieze are quite geometric, as if influenced by Italian Renaissance design, but the carving has an Arabic asymmetry to it, as do the drawer decoration and iron escutcheon around the keyhole.

10

9

9. A Charles II Oak Low Dresser, c1670

From its earliest origins in the medieval period, the dresser had a ceremonial function as an early sideboard. A dictionary of 1611 defined it as 'a court cupboard only to set a plate upon', and early accounts of court life describe how a gong was sounded to summon courtiers to the dresser before the strict ceremony of carrying dishes to the master of the house.

Elsewhere in Europe, the dresser was often painted and highly decorated, although many of the earliest examples through the 16th century would have been covered with tapestries or cloths. Originally carved, by the late 17th century the decoration was generally simple, as seen here. The dresser would have sat against a wall in the hall, with dishes and jugs of pewter, etc, sitting on it. It may have had a set of shelves attached to the wall above it – a basic form of Welsh dresser, in fact. Low dressers were generally made of oak, and sometimes yew.

From the 18th century onward, many dressers had an attached structure for shelves, closer to the dresser of today. It also became a more informal piece of furniture, found in the kitchen rather than the hallway.

10. A Louis XIV Lacquer and Boulle *Bureau Mazarin*, c1670

The elaborate decoration, bright colours and gilt work associated with Louis XIV's reign had in fact been popular for some time before his succession as ruler in 1661 at the age of 23. After the Renaissance influence decreased in France at the end of the 16th century, it fell to Henry IV (1589–1610) to re-establish the furniture industry by importing foreign craftsmen and setting up workshops in Paris. Under Louis XIII, Mme de Medici brought an Italian influence to the French court, combined with an interest in Flemish art. The flamboyant Italian style was reinforced by Cardinal Mazarin, himself an Italian, who ruled as Regent for the child Louis XIV from 1643–61.

Cardinal Mazarin gave his name to the eight-legged *bureau*, a form which later developed curved sides. The *bureau Mazarin* was invented in the second half of the 17th century, and was at first used as both a writing desk and a console table. This example is relatively light compared to many pieces, but is typically ostentatious with its lacquer and boulle decoration. The use of lacquer was promoted by Louis XIV's Minister of Arts, Colbert, after he formed the *Compagnie des Indes* in 1664. Through the company he imported lacquer and other art works from the Orient.

1600-1700

11. An Italian Baroque Marble-topped Side Table, *c*1670

One of a pair of high Baroque side tables from the Palazzo Massimo in Rome, this example boasts an impressive combination of colour, vigorous curves and lines pointing in all directions. The top is made of Siena marble, which creates its own pattern by variety of shade and colour, and its supporting frame consists entirely of curving lines. The legs bow, the stretchers curve in six different directions before meeting at the centre, and the apron is decorated with foliage and plumes. The contrast between the gilding and red paint is also dramatic; the table is the epitome of the Italian Baroque spirit, truly *con brio* (literally, 'with noise').

High Baroque was at its peak between 1630 and 1680 and was centred on Rome; the sculptural vogue was strong – this was the heyday of the renowned papal sculptor, Gianlorenzo Bernini (1598–1680). Papal influence exerted itself in other ways, too; an increase in wealth among new merchant dynasties brought life to the furniture trade, and nepotism saw the rise of several powerful families, including the Barbérini, Borghese, and Rezzonico families. The latter were based at the Palazzo Rezzonico in Venice, where the established sculptor, Antonio Corradini (1668–1752), carved much of their furniture.

12. A Charles II Oak Gate-leg Table, *c*1670

Charles II reigned for 25 years (1660–85) following the Puritan Protectorate, led by Oliver Cromwell. This table clearly shows the Puritan influence on design, with plain lines and a total lack of carved decoration. The shapes are geometric – the top is round, the stretchers rectangular – and even the turned legs are simple. The only decorative elements are minimal – the aprons hanging from the frieze.

This table has two single gate legs, one on each side, and a drawer in the frieze. The advantage of two flaps is that the table folds away to a small size. Tables such as these were made for a variety of purposes, from card playing to dining, and in a variety of sizes. The Windsor Castle accounts of the 1680s refer to 'an ovall wanscott table 6′ 6″ long and 4′ 6″ broad with a turned frame (the table made to fould)' supplied by one William Cleere.

After 1660, most tables were made in oak, although some were walnut, some yew, and in the countryside some of fruitwoods. The fashion for formal gate-leg tables died away in the early 18th century, but saw a revival after 1770 or so; they continued to be produced up to the mid 19th century, especially for country and common use.

12

11

13

13. A Charles II Oyster-veneered Table, c1670

This unusual decoration of small circles of veneer (hence the term 'oyster') is produced by cutting the branches of a tree across the grain. Like trunks, branches show annual growth rings, and an economical way of making the most of a special tree was to slice the branches and enclose the rings in a frame of lighter wood. This was generally found on English furniture, with woods as varied as laburnum, lignum vitae, olive-wood and various fruitwoods. The shape of this table is standard for the period, with barley-twist legs, inward curving cross-framed stretchers and bun feet.

From the 1680s onward, English furniture was marked by a return to decoration after Puritan plainness. There were strong influences from the court of Louis XIV, and William of Orange was accompanied by Dutch craftsmen, including Daniel Marot (1663–1752), when he came to the English throne in 1688. As a result, English cabinetmaking became truly European, blossoming with a new interest in decorative styles.

Inlay and marquetry were highly popular, using techniques such as 'seaweed' marquetry (made from very fine panels of marquetry resembling strands of seaweed), floral panels, and ivory and tortoiseshell inlay. In France at this time, André-Charles Boulle was developing the brass and tortoiseshell inlay that was named after him.

1600-1700

14. An English William and Mary Gilt Side Table, *c*1690

Originally from the Dutch royal family, William of Orange came to the throne of England through his marriage to Mary, the daughter of James II. He reigned from 1688 to 1694, bringing with him a greater European influence in the area of design than had ever been seen before in England. This influence was from two main sources: the French court style of Louis XIV (1643-1715), which became increasingly gilded and ornate as the century progressed; and Daniel Marot, the famous Huguenot craftsman who was William's main adviser on interior decorating (Marot had fled French persecution of the Protestants in the 1680s and taken up residence in Holland).

The rich combination of Dutch, Flemish and French influence can be seen on this table in terms of its ornateness. The table top is elaborately carved in relief with a cartouche, a departure from the English tradition of plain, functional tables which probably would have been covered with a cloth. The deep frieze has rows of lobes (rope-twists motifs) that were commonly found on Italian *cassoni* (marriage chests) and other Renaissance furniture. The legs are four 'S' scrolls, a change from the usual English turned, round-sectioned or barley-twists legs.

15. A Baroque Gilt Side Table, *c*1695

The full repertoire of Baroque decoration can be found on this side table. It is designed to take a heavy marble top (although this is possibly too slight to be the original), and wild foliate scrolls bearing unusual figures hang from the apron. There is also a figure in the centre of the cross-framed stretcher; holding a sheaf of corn, she may represent Ceres, the Roman corn goddess, or simply be an allegory of summer.

In the 17th century, sculptural allegories – and their application to furniture – were a popular Baroque feature. Consider the two main figures on the front legs of this table. On the left, another Ceres-types figure is dressed in classical drapes, representing summer, and on the right, a shivering, bearded man symbolizes winter. The likelihood is that this is one of a pair of console tables: the other would have shown spring, probably as a young girl with flowers, and autumn most likely would have been personified as Bacchus, the god of wine.

The origin of this table is not clear, particularly as some restoration work may have occurred on the front figures. The carving of the man, with his narrow Alpine face and the naturalistic branch beneath his arm, suggests Northern Europe: naturalism was characteristic of those countries. But generally big, scrolling Baroque tables are thought of as Italian. Established trade routes between Germany and Italy had been functioning since the Middle Ages, and so had the exchange of design ideas. This table probably comes from Austria, southern Germany or northern Italy, all of which, thanks to shifting national boundaries, shared similar styles.

16. A Boulle Table Top, *c*1695

The art of boulle (or 'buhl') work was named after its inventor, André-Charles Boulle (1642–1732). He was the most celebrated cabinetmaker during the reign of Louis XIV, and from 1662 onward he worked continuously for the royal family refurbishing the various palaces, especially Versailles. He originally trained as a cabinetmaker, architect, engraver and bronze worker, and published a series of engravings which helped to promote his work throughout Europe. Boulle never signed his pieces, and despite the fact that they sold for several thousands of pounds, a vast sum then, he was often in debt, thanks to his passion for collecting works of art: his enthusiasm for Renaissance art plunged him from surplus into crippling debt on several occasions, from which the King repeatedly protected him, much to his annoyance.

His technique used a combination of metals and tortoiseshell worked in one of two basic ways. *Première-partie* utilized background sheets of red or dark tortoiseshell decorated, through cut-outs, with underlays of various metals (including brass, pewter and copper). *Contre-partie*, as seen here, reversed the process, with a background of metal and tortoiseshell underlay. Boulle work remained popular in France from this time on, peaking in the 18th century and experiencing a revival in the 19th.

One of its disadvantages is that it damages easily; as the different metals expand at different rates, the work can lift off the table surface and is very difficult to replace. The wrinkle across the central oval has been caused in this way, but this is still a very fine example of 17th-century boulle work, showing a wealth of decoration: the central armorial, mythological figures, strapwork, floral and scroll inlay, and engraving all enhance the medley of bright colours.

14

16

15

1700
TO
1800

A gilt bronze mount from a bureau plat by Charles Cressent of c1730. Gilt mounts were popular in France from the last few decades of the 17th century onwards.

Charles Cressent (1685–1768) was France's most talented cabinet maker of the Régence period, working for the regent Duc d'Orléans and becoming the official royal cabinetmaker. His influence was in the move toward lighter furniture in the late 17th century; the 'commode Cressent' named after him is a mark of this influence.

Whereas the 17th century had been marked by its vast variety of table shapes and adornments, the 18th century was distinguished for its craftsmanship. Indeed, the 1700s saw a quality of manufacture never since equalled, with the added introduction of American craftsmen and designers as a force to be reckoned with.

André-Charles Boulle and his colleagues working at the court of Louis XV now preferred a lightening of structure and simplification of form, resulting in straighter lines and plain surfaces, foregoing inlay and tight curves on every edge. It is only necessary to look at French Régence styles, encompassing the first three decades of the century, to see how strong the reaction against decoration was in France, a moderate stance which enabled that country to avoid the fate that befell the ponderous Italian Baroque.

By 1730 in France a variety of tables was an essential and valued part of the furniture of the aristocratic household. During the Régence period there had been an increasing interest in the quality of manufacture as the range of decorative options declined. Stretchers were disappearing, and veneering with plain wood grain and lacquering was on the rise. In no time a new style, of which Régence is considered the first phase, fully emerged – Rococo – based on natural forms, such as shells and foliage, arranged asymmetrically. This light, elegant yet vibrant style quickly spread from France all over Europe. Because of the Rococo aversion to straight lines (which do not appear in nature), cabinetmakers were faced with the problem of making tables which curved in several different directions. On top of this, clients still wanted the same high standard of opulent veneering covering the wooden carcasses.

All these demands were met – and the highest of standards maintained – by gifted French *menuisiers* and *ébénistes* such as Charles Cressent (1685–1768) and Bernard van Risenburgh (fl. 1730–70), and, together with their fellow craftsmen – the mount-makers, gilders, etc – they brought about a golden age of furniture making. The new look for tables favoured eccentric curving, light-hearted constructions in light-coloured woods (often with parts cut out) and, especially in France, finely chiselled gilt-bronze, or ormolu, mounts. More table types were developed in France, notably small specialist ones such as the *table en chiffonière* (a work table with a high gallery) and the *table à ouvrage*, for needleworkers.

The Rococo in Italy and Germany essentially followed the lead of France, but in England there grew an affection for plain, dark woods, a trend which began in the 1600s with the Britons' love for their native walnut, and continued later with furniture made of dark red-brown mahogany, available from the colonies without any export duty after 1720. The new wood carved easily and also yielded beautiful grain patterns, known as 'figuring'. The Chippendale style developed, with Rococo patterns applied to a plethora of English tables – among the favoured motifs were leaf carving, pierced latticework and Chinese motifs. As an extension of this fantasy element, the Gothic style was revived; a medieval cathedral could be evoked on a table, whose legs might be carved as clusters of architectonic columns beneath arches in the structure's frieze.

Indeed there had been pattern-books of designs for furniture in the past – Nicolas Pineau, for example, produced Rococo designs in France, and William Kent's English Baroque patterns had been published in 1744 – but when Thomas Chippendale (1718–1799) published his *Gentleman and Cabinetmaker's Director* in 1754, containing over 200 designs, the English Rococo style was suddenly known and available all over Europe and North America – and many of the patterns contained within were for tables. Although there were many other pattern-books, the early acceptance of Chippendale's designs started a new vogue for 'Anglomania' in Europe; it also set the precedent for American cabinetmakers to copy later (post-1780) Hepplewhite and Sheraton table designs from their pattern-books well into the 19th century.

In France and England in the 1760s and 1770s, there was a sudden reaction against the light-hearted furniture of the Rococo era: tables were now being designed in the neo-Classical style, which had been popularized by the architect Robert Adam (1728–1792), who had toured Roman monuments and borrowed Classical architectural details for his interiors. In Adam designs, tables often played a crucial part, frequently being fixed near windows, thus giving symmetry to the formal room layouts. Rococo curves and the frippery of sculpted shells disappeared, and new straight lines characterized the tables of 1780s Britain – perhaps with the added enhancement of fluted legs emulating the columns which supported the roofs of Roman temples. The tops and aprons of tables tended to be flatter, often of plain mahogany or with restrained, geometric inlay; cabriole legs and hoof feet also disappeared toward the end of the century. France and the rest of Europe looked to England's example and therefore toned down the elaborate decoration and colour of their tables. The application of ormolu mounts continued, tempered, however, by the restraints of neo-Classicism. With the French Revolution, the furniture trade slowed down; without new orders from royal clients, the quality of work fell slightly.

Around 1700 American settlers used either tables brought from their homelands in Europe or, as was more often the case, made them of native woods in the style of the Old World. Since early Americans were preoccupied with living rather than luxury, furniture design in the colonies, essentially following European trends, of necessity lagged behind considerably. Thus in New England, English styles of 1690 were still current in 1710, and Queen Anne style tables were popular in 1750, nearly four decades after that monarch's reign. On the whole, simple but elegant plainness appealed to the Puritan spirit of the settlers for some time, but by the 1780s and 1790s, after gaining independence from Europe – and thanks to Chippendale's pattern-books and to increased emigration – colonial table production began to catch up with the Old World and in fact develop its own distinctive character. By 1800 North America boasted thriving centres of high-quality production of European-style tables with local variations, such as different styles of inlay and ball-and-claw feet. These cabinetmaking hubs were concentrated in Philadelphia, New England and New York; in the latter, Duncan Phyfe was one of the best-known producers of Federal tables, some of which still bear his original label.

17. An Italian Gilt Side Table, *c*1700

The strong Italian sculptural tradition meant that most artists and craftsmen could turn their hand to carving decoration. This table is similar to pieces by Filippo Juvarra (1678–1736), who worked in the Palazzo Reale, Turin, in the 1730s. But it is often difficult to date furniture produced between the end of the 17th century and the beginning of the 18th – as a whole, it is grandiose, gilt and scrolling. Italy clearly led the way in design during this period, but despite this the quality of workmanship was not often high.

The carving on the table support uses natural forms, such as the central scallop shell, thus demonstrating the roots of the Rococo movement, which was to emerge fully between 1730 and 1750. The legs are scrolling, dolphin-like forms, and the support seems rather large for the small marble top. The likelihood is that the top is not original to the piece: as good seams of marble are increasingly rare and usually limited, it was often difficult to replace a smashed top with marble of the same quality.

18. An English Yew Table, *c*1710

The use of yew for this table, made during the reign of Queen Anne (1702–14), was an unusual alternative to walnut, the preferred wood until 1720. After that date, a relaxation of import duty from English colonies allowed mahogany to be bought more cheaply and competitively, and so it became used in greater amounts. With a tightly patterned grain and a bright yellow-gold colour, the yew provides a subtle accompaniment to the simple shape of the table.

The top is inlaid with the design of a house, an example of the interest in homely motifs – hunting, country life, etc – in the Queen Anne period. It is surrounded by a cushioned edge, another Queen Anne feature, above an undecorated frieze, and is supported by straight legs ending in pad feet. There is no stretcher, which gives a lighter feel to the table, and the only ornament is a slight scroll where the leg joins the apron. Even the scroll seems restrained compared to the earlier fussy Baroque scroll, and it is this air of understatement and subtlety which characterizes Queen Anne furniture.

18

19

20

19. A French Régence *Table à Gibier*, *c*1720
20. A French Régence Side Table, *c*1720

1700-1800

The term *Régence* specifically refers to the early years of Louis XV of France's reign. On the death of Louis XIV in 1715, a Regent was appointed to rule the country until Louis XV came of age. In furniture, however, Regence style covers the first few decades of the 18th century, and shows a reaction against the heavier, more ornate furniture of Louis XIV's reign from 1643 to 1715.

With the *table à gibier,* the stretcher remains heavy and square-sectioned, but the square edges of the top are slightly rounded, and the architectural, square-sectioned legs curve, which give a lighter feel. The table's frieze is ornate, as on earlier tables, and is decorated with scallop shells from which pierced foliate scrolls extend.

The Régence side table dates from a few years later, and shows clear signs of Rococo influence in its tapering legs and lighter, curved stretchers. The deeper frieze on the top gives the piece a vertical feel which makes it seem taller than it actually is, and the restrained decoration makes it feel lighter.

21. An Italian Gilt Wood Side Table, *c*1720

Figure sculpture has always been part of the Italian artistic tradition. In consequence, Italian tables are more often supported by human figures than those from any other country. One of a pair, this table shows considerable High Baroque influence. Overall, it seems fairly heavy, and is vaguely in the style of Antonio Corradini, who worked in the early 18th century. A sculptor, Corradini carved some of the furniture for the Palazzo Rezzonico in Venice, and specialized in beautiful human and mythological figures, sea monsters and angels in the Baroque style. He was already a well-known and highly rewarded sculptor of his time, and it is a reflection of the importance placed on figural work that he, not a furniture carver, was chosen for this important commission.

This table is clearly a side table intended to be set against a wall, as the two rear legs are decorated in front only.

22. A French Régence Oak Console Table, *c*1720

By the end Louis XIV's reign in 1715, almost all courtly furniture in France was gilded. During the reign of Louis XV, much design was still influenced by his predecessor, who was known as the Sun King because of his passion for gilt and other visual extravagances. However, France had long had a tradition of carved, natural wood, which had flourished at the beginning of the century under Louis XIII (1610–43) and the Government of Cardinal Mazarin. Throughout the reign of Louis XV, the two different styles developed, as can be seen clearly on this table.

Made of oak and one of a pair, this bare wood table has been carved with courtly mask decorations, an ornate frieze and heavy, square-sectioned stretchers. Originally it may have been gilt, but it has since been stripped, perhaps during the 19th century (it was unusual, however, for gilded furniture to be made of a dense wood such as oak, which is harder to carve than a softwood). It is unlikely that the marble top seen here is the original; that probably would have been a more finely patterned marble of more exotic colours.

23. A pair of French Régence Painted *Torchères* and a Blackamoor *Guéridon*, *c*1725

Torchères such as these were used to augment the main lighting of a room in a similar way to a spotlight today. The chief source of light would have been in the form of a chandelier (literally, candleholder) or sconces (wall-mounted candle brackets). This substantial pair are cream-painted, heightened with gilt and feature sculptural carving. They are probably made of a softwood, such as beech, and are in the Régence style – popular in France and England in the first few decades of the 18th century.

The blackamoor is a 19th-century copy of a late 17th- or early 18th-century Italian or French figure. Although purely decorative here, an original would have held a candlestand in place of the basket of fruit. Black pages were very fashionable in 17th-century courts around the Mediterranean and were generally recruited from the Moors, the Arabic-Berber races from North Africa. There was supposedly a servant called *Guéridon* who gave his name to such candlestands, and which was later applied to any small round table.

25

22

23

24

24. A Louis XV Ebony Table, c1725

This chic and elegant table from the time of Louis XV uses the classic combination of ebony veneer, ormolu mounts and brass stringing. It is the stark contrast of colours which gives the table its particular style (a look often associated with this date of French furniture), and the lack of stretchers contributes to its lightness. The black veneer manages to both slim down the already slender cabriole legs and give weight to the top.

The French Régence period in furniture refers to the first few decades of the 18th century. It saw a sharp reaction against the heavy, over-decorated pieces of the end of the 17th century, as seen in the bulbous, colourful work of André-Charles Boulle.

25. A French Régence Ebonized *Bureau Plat*, c1725

The *bureau plat* was the leading form of writing table in the Régence period, whose styles prevailed over the first quarter of the century. Earlier 17th-century writing tables were generally eight-legged, with a deep frieze and three vertical drawers. This cubic design was epitomized by the work of the French architect/designer, Jean Bérain (1638–1711).

Around the turn of the century, the simpler *bureau plat* was introduced, replacing earlier heavy, boulle (inlaid brass and tortoiseshell) pieces. This table is ebonized, using paint and polish to resemble ebony. The mounts are ormolu, but functional rather than decorative, and the top is tooled leather.

Régence was the French style of c1720, not to be confused with the English Regency period of c1810.

26. An English George I Gilt Side Table, c1725

Following the sobriety of design during the reign of Queen Anne, the arrival of the new Hanoverian dynasty brought an explosion of colour and taste. This table is a classic George I piece, decorated with organic shapes of leaves and scrolls, and with strapwork carved in low relief.

To achieve the effect of gilded low-relief carving, tables such as these were manufactured in gilt gesso. This process involved making a table in a softwood, such as pine or beech, to the approximate shape and size required, and then coating it with gesso – a paste made of chalk dust bound with parchment size (or glue). When dried, the gesso was carved in low relief to form strapwork or other patterns, and then gilded. Strapwork had been common since c1550 in Europe, and was often in relief on 'salmon spawn' – a plain gilt background punched with hundreds of tiny dots.

Identical to a table originally owned by the British Royal Family, this piece is stamped with three indistinct initials under its apron. It is in the style of James Moore (d.1726), who was cabinetmaker to the Crown and who supplied furniture to London's Kensington Palace.

27. A French Gilt Wood Side Table, after a design by Nicolas Pineau, c1730

This table epitomizes the French Rococo style with its complex composition of scrolls and curves, of diagonal, horizontal and vertical lines, and of sculpture and decoration. Despite its many components, it is quite elegant, particularly when compared to much Italian Rococo.

Nicolas Pineau (1684–1754) was influential in the promotion of French Rococo in many fields, including architecture and jewellery, and spent some time in Russia working on royal palaces around St. Petersburg. On his return to Paris in 1726, he published a book of engraving designs for furniture and interiors which frequently employed rocaille motifs such as shells and flowers. His speciality was arranging these asymmetrically, a style which he was the first to introduce.

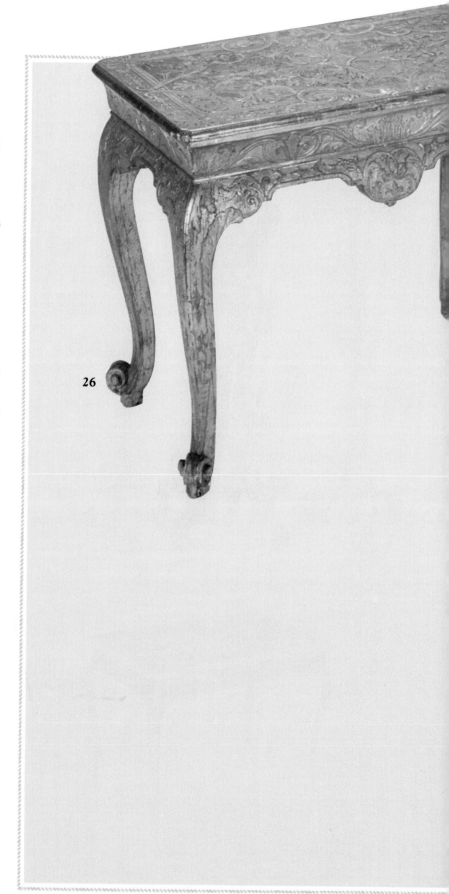

26

27

28. An English George II Console Table by William Kent, c1730

This is one of a pair of console tables in the Italian-influenced style which Kent (1684–1748) and his friend and patron, the 3rd Earl of Burlington (1685–1753), were largely responsible for in the first half of 18th-century England. Of heavy, often gilt and richly carved wood, Kent's furniture was based on Italian Baroque work and is known as Palladian, after the work of the Italian architect, Andrea Palladio (1508–80).

Kent himself began his career as an apprentice coach-painter, but was sent to train in Italy as an artist on several occasions. There, he met Lord Burlington and the two went on to become arbiters of English taste and fashion in the 1720s and 1730s. Kent worked as a painter, sculptor, architect, interior decorator and landscape gardener, although his chief influence was on architecture and the decorative arts. He was responsible for the design of London's Horse Guards Parade, and worked on the interior of Kensington Palace. Not everyone was impressed by his work, however. Referring to his painting, the artist William Hogarth dismissed him as a 'contemptible dauber', and Horace Walpole spoke of his work as 'immeasurably ponderous', although he also mentioned that its overall effect was 'audacious, splendid and audacious'.

29. A Louis XV Walnut Console Table, c1735

Asymmetry was a crucial element of Rococo design. Applied to furniture, this meant that neither the two sides nor the top or bottom of a piece bore identical shapes. If a 17th century table, for example, was divided down the middle, the two parts would be mirror images. Here, that is clearly not the case. The cartouche in the centre of the frieze is not symmetrical, nor is the ornamented stretcher. The table top is as far from being rectangular, and is obviously of greater weight than its base. Another type of symmetry, although less precise, compares the visual 'weight' or mass of an object. Typically, the heavy top of a 17th-century bureau is balanced 'symmetrically' by the 'weight' of heavy scrolling stretchers.

This style of furniture is sometimes called *con brio*, which translates as 'noisily' (in music it means 'with movement'). The table is walnut, a rich wood that is easily carved, and the decoration is rocaille – motifs taken from nature, as opposed to the classical, architectural motifs seen in the 17th century.

30. A Louis XV Gilt Iron Console Table, c1740

Mainland Europe – France in particular – has a lively tradition of fine ironwork, which started in the 16th century and continues up to today. Iron stretchers on tables were in use in Spain as early as the 17th century, although Great Britain and the United States only adopted the idea of metal furniture in the 19th and 20th centuries.

This console table and its iron leg supports use hammered-steel strips to form a single cabriole leg. The pierced frieze imitates wood-carving, but allowed craftsmen greater freedom to experiment because of the strength of metal. The decoration here is not hammered or wrought when hot, like the frame, but made from a separate, thinner sheet of metal which is more pliable. The scallop shell and pendent flowers have been cut out as silhouettes and bent into shape using a gentle applied heat.

31. A Louis XV Console Table, c1740

This is a good example of a Rococo gilt wood and gesso console table. The console table originated from the reign of Louis XIV – the *Galerie des Glaces* (Gallery of Mirrors) at the Palais de Versailles is lined with them, alternating between windows and mirrors along the walls – and was at that time fairly square in shape, with straight, square-sectioned members.

This piece, however, is pure Rococo. All curves and very asymmetrical, its legs taper inward and its stretcher bears a highly elaborate, floral design. Much of the decoration is rocaille (motifs taken from nature), a reaction against the solid, monumental design of the Baroque-influenced 17th century.

32. A Louis XV *Table à Ouvrage*, c1745

The name *table à ouvrage* ('work table') often refers to needlework tables such as this one. The top is leather-covered, as are the drawers, which held scissors, thread, etc, and the table is decorated with elaborate Rococo inlay designs of organic motifs in kingwood.

This would have been considered the height of Rococo taste, restrained but lively. Pieces such as this were produced by the cabinetmakers. Bernard Van Risenburgh, who worked between 1730–1770 and stamped his work 'B.V.R.B.' (and whose identity was only revealed in 1957), and Roger Vandercruse, known as Lacroix (1728–99), who used the stamp 'R.V.L.C.'.

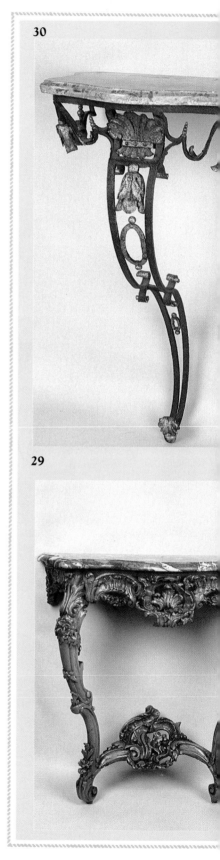

30

29

28

32

31

33. One of a Pair of Chinese K'ang, or Low, Tables, c1750

This low table stands only a few inches off the ground, and was made as an accompaniment for a K'ang (a Chinese low platform), from which it takes its name. The K'ang was in use as early as the Han dynasty (c200 BC), and consisted of a central rectangular section supported on a structure of frames. K'angs were used for both sleeping and sitting; when sitting, the K'ang table, as seen here, was placed on the K'ang (platform), which was at the right height for reading or writing.

K'angs and K'ang tables were generally made of rosewood, carved out of as few pieces of wood as possible. They were usually very simple, using no nails or dowels, but instead disguised mortice-and-tenon joints. Lacquer, made from the sap of trees, was popular as a defence against damp and insects, as it dried to a hard resinous finish. The lacquer was then often decorated with incised designs, and sometimes gilt or set with ivory inlay. Other tables used by the Chinese included square or round versions for eating, and high rectangular tables set against a wall as a stand for a *ch'in* (or lute).

The lacquer decoration on these tables became a highly refined art form in the East, and the source of inspiration for European chinoiserie decoration from the 16th century onward.

34. A Finnish Pine Dresser, c1750

This table with a cupboard below comes from the National Museum of Finland in Helsinki. It is the legacy of a medieval model which continued to be made well into the 18th and 19th centuries for everyday use, despite the fact that the Renaissance arrived in Scandinavia in the 16th and 17th centuries (brought by artists, such as Albrecht Dürer (1471–1528), who travelled widely around Europe spreading Italian styles. The continued popularity of traditional forms was due to a lack of tools and money, which meant that pieces needed to be strictly functional.

The uneven top and edges are proof that the timber was cut with a primitive saw and an adze probably was used in shaping the pieces, which were then pegged together. As this would have been one of very few pieces of furniture in a home, it would have performed a variety of functions – as a table, seating, storage for valuables and food, etc. It is clearly the basis for some of the forms of contemporary pine furniture produced today.

35

36

34

33

35. An Italian Rococo Console Table, *c*1750

This Italian version of a Louis XV console table would have served the same purpose as a French example: part of the integral decoration of a room, it would sit between or beneath windows, possibly with a mirror above it.

Painted rather than gilded, the motifs on this table are largely 'grotesque', taken from designs found in ancient Roman grottoes excavated from the 15th century onward. The unusual shapes were pounced on by enquiring 18th-century artists once the influence of Renaissance and Baroque designs wore thin. One such was the Renaissance artist, Raphael (1483–1520), who employed this grotesque style to decorate galleries in the Vatican in Rome.

So similar were grotesque motifs – shells, garlands of flowers, scrolling fungus-like forms and exaggerated curves – to those of the French Rococo rocaille repertoire, that it is unclear whether Rococo originated in France or Italy. French pieces tend to be more restrained, Italian more exuberant.

This table possibly originated in Genoa, in the north of Italy and near to the French border, and seems to combine the best characteristics of both versions – resulting in an elegant, original piece.

36. A Mid 18th century South German Card Table, *c*1750

This sculptural table shows the influence of the German Neuwied school of cabinetmaking, whose famous sons David and Abraham Roentgen were producing from their workshop from the mid 18th century onward. Sculptural wood-carving had long been a speciality of the region, reaching its zenith with religious Renaissance carving of *c*1500; subdued under the anti-Catholic Reformation movement in the 16th century, carving remains central to South German art to this day.

Made of walnut, the table has a marquetry top exhibiting several Rococo motifs – bell-flowers, garlands, even a parrot; the overall effect is somewhat darker and more architectural than that of English marquetry, although in both a variety of woods is used. The whole table has a slightly sculptural feel to it. The hoofed feet are typically South German, and the projecting rounded corners would have been hollowed out to support a candlestick when the table was open. The top unhinges from the centre to reveal the baize-covered playing surface.

37. A Mid 18th century German *Table à Ecrire, c1750*

This table is titled in French because of its obvious debt to French design. Germany at this date consisted of numerous small states and principalities rather than one unified country. This led to considerable regional variations in furniture design and quality of craftsmanship, one of several reasons why French fashions had so much influence. The Seven Years' War (1756–63), involving much of Europe, also led to a severe loss of Saxony's territory and income, which meant yet more reliance on France for furniture production.

This piece is discreetly Rococo, with gently curving legs and apron, and upturned toes. The German influence can be seen in the inlay and marquetry, less clear than French work and utilizing the unusual combination of kingwood, yew and amaranth. Although French craftsmen almost always marked their works, tight guild regulations in Germany left most pieces anonymous.

38. A Louis XV *Bureau Plat, c1750*

The *bureau plat*, introduced during the Régence period, proved very popular and became a standard form in French furniture. The finest examples of the 18th century are associated with the French cabinetmakers, Charles Cressent (1685–1768) and André-Charles Boulle (1642–1732); the latter was successful at adapting 17th-century designs to 18th-century tastes.

This example is relatively simple and severe in its line, but has definite Rococo asymmetrical tendencies. Its edges are curved, its legs cabriole, and the top is not rectangular. Veneered in a typically French herringbone pattern of tulipwood and kingwood, it is simply decorated with beautifully executed ormolu mounts. The mounts on a piece of furniture such as this would have been made by members of the guild of *ciseleurs*; the guild was devoted to working up bronze mounts before they were gilded.

39. A Louis XV Marquetry Small Table, *c1750*

During the second half of the century, the fashion for women to receive visitors while dressing led to the manufacture of numerous small, beautifully decorated occasional tables. These ranged from high tripod tables, which stood about 5ft (1.5m) high and held mirrors – used when standing to dress hair, especially in Italy – to small dressing tables such as this. Both practical and decorative, they were often finely finished with inlay and marquetry.

A good example of restrained Rococo, this table concentrates on shape rather than elaborate decoration. The legs are elegant and outswept, and the apron is in the form of a Cupid's bow. The frieze contains a brushing slide (which extends to hold brushes), and the lid lifts to reveal compartments for make-up, powders, combs, etc.

40. A Louis XV *Table de Nuit, c1750*

This simple and functional piece of furniture held a chamber pot and sat next to the bed. Night tables were used extensively throughout Europe during the second half of the century, and later models became increasingly sophisticated, using fake drawers and closing doors to disguise their real function.

Although this piece is from Louis XV's reign, which was renowned for ostentation, it is relatively discreet, discarding the earlier addiction to ormolu.

41. An English George III Chippendale Sideboard Table, *c1754*

The name 'sideboard table' comes from Thomas Chippendale (1718–79) himself, as first seen in his *Gentleman and Cabinet-maker's Director*, 1st edition, published in 1754. A guide to which cabinetmakers subscribed, a pattern-book such as Chippendale's provided a detailed drawing of a piece of furniture, giving a series of options for decoration: this allowed furniture makers to either copy or adapt the original idea. Plate LX in the first of Chippendale's three editions illustrates all the characteristics of this table, although the original drawing is slightly asymmetrical due to the different suggestions it puts forward.

The piece is typical of English Rococo tables, although its top is later than its other components, possibly due to damage. The frieze is covered in interlaced blind-fret cusps, an ogee and criss-cross ornamentation using foliate scrolls; its centre acanthus-leaf cartouche has an apron pendant hanging below. The table legs are elaborately Gothic, with a central column supported by four smaller columns, all joined by crocketed arches and ending in architectural feet.

This well-known sideboard table, which is discussed in Percy Macquoid's *The Age of Mahogany, 1720–1770*, is relatively modest in size (6ft 6in/198m wide) and would have stood against a wall to be used for serving. It falls between the more heavily constructed early 18th-century side tables and the lighter, more elaborate sideboards of George III's reign.

41

39

37

40

38

42. A Louis XV Table, c1755

This dignified table is plain by French standards. It is part of the general style which covered the move from Rococo furniture through transitional designs to the neo-classical influence. It shows very little decoration; there is no ormolu, and the inlay and cross-banding are both unobtrusive.

Rococo influence can be seen in the colour, shape (curved legs and bow apron) and lustre of the table, but the overall lines are distinctly more sobre, following a lead by Charles-Nicolas Cochin (1715–90), which he took in the late 1740s after touring classical Rome.

43. A Louis XV Tulipwood Writing Table, c1755

This table is from the transitional period between the Rococo and neo-Classical styles. The lightness, colour and curving lines are all Rococo, as are the asymmetrical cartouche on the top and the herringbone pattern created by the alternate stripes of light and dark tulipwood. The table's cabriole legs still curve, and the apron bows. But the cleaner lines of the neo-Classical period are here, and the ormolu decoration is not excessive.

The piece is probably from the Dubois, a dynasty of cabinetmakers established by Jacques Dubois (c1693–1763), and continued by his brother, Louis (1732–c1790), and nephew, René (1737–99). René worked for Louis XVI and Marie-Antoinette before opening a furniture shop in Paris in 1779.

44. A Louis XV *Coiffeuse*, c1755

During Louis XV's reign the frivolity of the French aristocracy reached a peak which is difficult to imagine today. The paintings of Jean-Honoré Fragonard (1732–1806) depict the indulgencies and excesses in both lifestyle and personal appearance of the rich. *The Swing* (c1766), for example, was commissioned by a baron for his mistress; Fragonard was requested to paint her on a swing being pushed by a bishop, with the baron in a place where he 'could have a good look at the legs'.

Elaborate hairstyles were all the rage, and a *coiffeuse* such as this was sat at to create them – the name is taken from the French verb *coiffer*, meaning to dress the head. The central panel of the top raises to reveal a mirror, flanked by compartments for make-up, powders, etc. The three frieze drawers are also compartmentalized, and the slide over the central drawer pulls out to hold brushes.

45. An 18th-century Florentine Scagliola Table Top, 1756

Scagliola is a man-made composition which imitates marble and other ornamental stones, and takes its name from the Italian *scaglia*, the number of small pieces of hard and semi-precious stones used in *pietra dura* work. It is made of finely grained plaster of Paris mixed with glue, and coloured as required. Traces have been found in ancient Roman artefacts, but the art was revived by Guido del Conte (1584–1649) and became very popular in the 18th century (it was almost always produced in Italy).

This beautiful table top is one of a signed pair, and in consequence is very rare indeed. It is inscribed 'D P Belloni A Florentia F 1756', or 'Don Pietro Belloni at Florence made this (F=fecit) 1756', and is of excellent quality. Showing the Rococo style at its best, it uses light colours, particularly pale blues and greens, and the border features flowers, scallop shells, small animals and human figures intertwined. The central rustic scene is typically romanticized – in reality, the life of an 18th-century shepherd was not so idyllic.

In England in 1664 the diarist John Evelyn wrote 'I have frequently wondered that we never practised this in England for cabinets', but it was first seen in the Royal Household in the 1670s. In 1790, scagiola was much in demand as a cheap way of imitating rare marble, and a factory producing it was opened in London. It was used by both Robert Adam and George Smith; the latter recommended it for the tops of small tables in his book, *Household Furniture*, of 1808.

42

43

45

44

46. An American Queen Anne Tray-top Table, *c*1760

This tray-top table is almost identical to a walnut tea table illustrated in the *Shorter Dictionary of English Furniture* by Ralph Edwards, dated 1715 (towards the end of Queen Anne's reign). The American table, however, has a skirt beneath the rectangular top with protruding apron, a late Queen Anne feature, and is made of cherry wood, which has a smooth grain and tends to be less finely figured. It was made in New England, probably Connecticut, where such skirting and pad feet were popular.

American cabinetmakers often used native fruit woods, which sometimes included walnut and mahogany, although it would be very rare for an English cabinetmaker to use cherry wood for a fine-quality piece such as this. Native English woods almost always indicate provincial manufacture. Queen Anne American furniture was made well into the 1760s, even though the monarch herself had died nearly 50 years earlier.

47. An Italian Louis XV *Lacca contrafatta* Side Table, *c*1760

Much Italian furniture in the 18th century was influenced by French artists, particularly in the northern areas of Piedmont and Liguria. On the whole, designs were slightly exaggerated – curves were greater, decoration more colourful – compared to the French pieces, and craftsmanship was often poorer.

In this case, the decoration on the table top is uniquely Italian. *Lacca contrafatta*, as it was known, consisted of printed paper cut-outs, often of rustic or Oriental figures. These were attached to furniture which had generally been painted with a cream or yellow base, and the whole surface was then varnished. The firm of Remondini, of Bassano del Grappa, was renowned for this style of work, which was cheaper and less difficult to produce than lacquer. A variety of Italian furniture ranging from bookcases to tea caddies was treated in this way. The technique is largely associated with Venice, but, as with other forms of lacquer, it was practised throughout northern Italy.

Also typically Italian is this table's sculptural quality: the Louis XV cabriole legs start with an angelic head at the top, and the feet are carved into leafy hooves. It has two tiers, and is a variant on the *chiffonière*, a table form which had space for books and often a drawer for needlework.

47

46

49

48

48. A Chinese Hardwood Altar Table, c1760

The use of tables had been fully established in China since the days of the T'ang Dynasty (AD618–906), although they served a different purpose to those in Europe. Often appearing in pairs, they would be set along a wall to hold incense burners or a *ch'in* (Chinese lute); in a formal room this would be on the east or west walls as the main entrance was always in the south wall, but in a less formal setting they may well have been placed asymmetrically. Generally, Chinese table models changed little over many centuries, although their decoration, as evidenced here, tended to increase as the years passed and Western influence grew.

The size of China meant that many woods were available, but among the most valued was *hua'li,* a hardwood similar to rosewood. In the south, bamboo was used, often varnished with lacquer to prevent damage from insects. On the whole, Chinese furniture followed simple, elegant lines made to fit together without dowel or nails. This high-quality piece shows an unusual amount of decoration, with extensive carving on the apron below the top. The top itself is pierced with a naturalistic design of the branches of the prunus tree, and the apron is dotted with prunus blossom inlay.

49. An English George III Occasional or Wine Table, c1760

In general, Georgian furniture fell into two main streams – the controlled, veneered pieces which were adapted from the popular pattern-books; and the more natural, flowing pieces which represented the originality and traditional craftsmanship of English 18th-century cabinetmaking at its best.

This small table belongs to the second category. Its charm comes from its own elegantly functional shape and simplicity, and does not rely on either a pattern book or a contrived setting to look its best. The wood is a good colour, and the top is simply decorated with a reeded dished edge, to prevent glasses from falling. It is also hinged, which allowed the snap top to fold down when not in 'occasional' use. The column is plain, with two small collars above the slender tripod, and the legs sweep gracefully down to the rounded pad feet with a small carved disc around each toe.

50. An American Chippendale Tea Table, *c*1760

The tilting top of this tea table is similar to that of its English cousin, and is released by a 'bird cage' mechanism – the latch is surrounded by tiny turned columns, like a cage. These are just visible at the top of the column support.

Made of finely figured walnut, it has a slight upturned edge to accommodate the crockery and is beautifully angular. The slender column has a knop known as a compressed ball and sharply curving cabriole feet. The ball-and-claw feet on this table have the pronounced shape typical of Philadelphia, and on the whole the piece is a refined, elegant example of that city's style.

51. Two French Bedside Tables, *c*1760

These two night tables are typically Rococo, with their swelling outlines, uneven curved galleries above the top, and asymmetrical ormolu mounts, castors and fine sabots.

The spaces were meant to hold chamber pots, and the handles on the left-hand example and spaces on the right-hand one are for carrying the tables. Nicolas Petit (1732–91) made the table on the right. A successful Parisian businessman, he both made and sold furniture in his workshops in Faubourg St-Antoine, marking both his and other works he sold with his stamp.

52. A Transitional *Guéridon, c*1760

Although the word *guéridon* referred to a tall candlestand in the 17th century, by the middle of the 1700s it was used to describe a small round table such as this. It is in the transitional style, derived from the more extreme Rococo, with legs that gently curve from a pointed 'knee' just under the frieze. It is made of tulipwood with herringbone crossbanding.

Note the return of the stretcher, here used as a second tier. It is not structurally necessary for a table of this design, and has been introduced for decoration. The source of transitional table design is clear: from Louis XV in the 1740s to Louis XVI in the 1780s.

52

53

51

50

53. A Louis XV *Table à la Bourgogne, c1760*

The mid 18th century saw a fascination for gadgetry in furniture, both in France and England. The future Louis XVI of France had a considerable influence on furniture design long before his succession to the throne in 1774. He was particularly interested in technical design and mechanical devices, an interest shared by the Georgians in England, as seen in their writing desks.

When closed, this table appears quite ordinary, with a deep frieze. When opened, however, a fitted interior with four small drawers and compartments for writing utensils pops up, and the leather-lined flap provides a writing surface. Also known as a *secrétaire à capucin*, this form was often associated with the Parisian cabinetmaker, Roger Vandercruse, known as Lacroix. A fine example of his work from around the same date can be seen in the Musée Nissim de Camondo in Paris.

54. An American Chippendale Tea Table, *c1765*

This table comes from New England, and is strikingly similar to English tea tables from the end of George II's reign, c1750. Its simple, dignified form, circular top, turned column and tripod base are all European features. It is made of mahogany, the favoured English wood of the time, and is probably from Boston, Massachusetts, which was – and still is – proud of its English heritage, and whose cabinetmakers were keen to emulate English styles.

In Boston, for example, chair backs are found as direct copies of the work of Chippendale and Robert Mainwaring. Two other distinct Boston characteristics are the decoration on the knees of the cabriole legs – a Rococo scrolling style made with a punch rather than carved with a chisel – and the rat-claw feet, broadened to look more like a rat's paw than a lion's (as with ball-and-claw feet).

54

55. An American Chippendale Mixing Table, *c*1765

The contrast between the harmonious curves of the stand and patterned marble top of this table is striking. Although marble-topped tables had been popular since the 16th century in Europe, a combination of a crude slab and walnut such as this is unlikely to be found in English furniture of the same date. It is unusual in European furniture to find marble combined with anything other than a lightly decorated and coloured base of gilt or painted wood which complements the natural formation of the stone. In America, however, marble was highly valued and thought of as exotic.

Known as a slab-top table, this piece was commissioned by Benjamin Franklin for his daughter (according to family tradition), and is still in the family. The marble is Pennsylvanian, and the base is typical of Philadelphia cabinetmaking – with its undulating apron, long cabriole legs with tightly clasping ball-and-claw feet, and a carved scallop shell on each knee. The retention of the shell from the Queen Anne period was characteristic of Philadelphia work, particularly carved in this naturalistic way.

56. A Louis XV *Guéridon, c*1765

This small round table shows the standard marks of the neo-classical style. It has a pierced brass gallery around both tiers, the straight edges of the drawer front are emphasized with ormolu, and the legs, rather than being cabriole, are virtually straight with a bend in them.

It was probably made by Roger Vandercruse (1728–1799), who was better known as Lacroix and who stamped his work 'R LACROIX' or 'R.V.L.C.'. He was from a family of cabinetmakers, headed by his Flemish father, François Vandercruse. Three of his five sisters married well-known cabinetmakers, (the eldest married first Jean-François Oeben and then Jean-Henri Reisener, another Simon Oeben, and the third, Simon Guillaume), his brother was a master clockmaker, and his son, Pierre, became a *maître ébéniste*.

This table is also very similar to the work of Charles Topino (1742-1803), who excelled at making small pieces of furniture. His use of marquetry was often highly original, with his trademark garlands and foliage often repeated in the ormolu mounts. He worked for nobility, dealers and fellow craftsmen.

57. A Louis XV Transitional Console Table, *c*1765

French design dominated world furniture fashions throughout the reigns of Louis XIV and XV, moving from the heavy Baroque styles at the beginning of the period to lighter, more elegant Rococo by the end. By 1760, French influence was waning, and England emerged as a new influence. Toward the end of the century, the dominant style, restrained and neo-classical, was the very opposite of Rococo.

This table comes from the transitional period between the two, and combines elements of both. The legs, for instance, still curve but are definitely straightening. The symbols on the frieze and stretcher are swags, festoons and urns – all classical motifs. But the table as a whole is moulded into the shape of a Rococo console table.

During the mid 18th century, many European designers travelled to Italy to study the emerging neo-classical styles. These included the Englishman, Robert Adam, who studied in Rome in the 1770s, the Marquis de Marigny, Madame de Pompadour's brother and Charles-Nicolas Cochin from France in 1749. Cochin (1715–90) was later to become Director General of Buildings in France and championed a return to 'the way of good taste of the preceding century'.

58. A Louis XV Reading Table, *c*1765

This stunning example of craftsmanship is unattributed, although it was possibly made by Léonard Boudin (known to have worked on similar pieces), perhaps with marquetry by Gerreit Jensen, renowned for his sophistication and use of ivory. There is a table of the same type in the Louvre in Paris, stamped by Christophe Wolff. A number of other craftsmen were working to this remarkably high standard around this date: Jean-François Oeben was known for his inlay pictures, and J-C Delafosse published a book of marquetry designs in the 1760s.

This table, which opens to reveal three sliding panels for reading, writing, etc, shows two strands of influence: its roots lie in the Rococo movement, with its curved outline and marquetry pictures of landscapes and mythological scenes in mother-of-pearl, ivory and wood. But it also shows neo-Classical dignity in its elegant legs, which although curved are almost straight; its curved top, which is fundamentally rectangular; and its inlay on the legs of husks and geometric florets. These contradictions are characteristic of the so-called transitional period between Rococo and neo-Classicism during which the table was made.

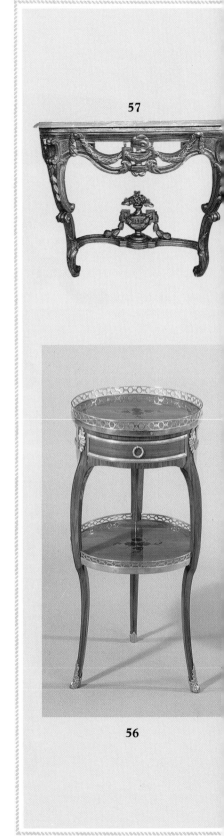

57

56

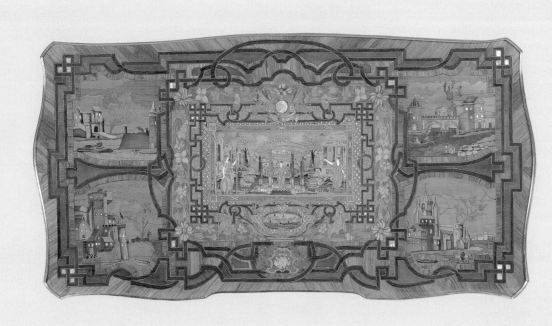

58

55

59. A Rosewood Writing Table by Thomas Chippendale, c1765

This beautiful table is rare, both because of its remarkable kidney shape and because all the documents surrounding its original sale from Thomas Chippendale to one Winifred Constable still survive. That invoice, 'to a large horseshoe table of black rosewood neatly inlaid with other woods and in a neat frame at £10 10s (10 guineas)', also specifies a damask leather cover at 18s; 89½ft (27.3m) of packing case at 3d a foot, total £1 2s 3d; and deal, screw and packing for 4s 6d. The total for the order was £12 14s 9d.

Chippendale is known to have spent much time working in the large house at Burton Constable for which this table was made. The house has spectacular bay windows, and the table may well have been designed to fit one of them, hence its unusual shape. It is discreet and uncluttered by Chippendale standards, its decoration relying on the contrast of grains and the inlaid fan-shaped patterns linked by a single line of husks. This motif is repeated on the tapering legs.

In many ways, the table is similar to furniture of mid-century France, concentrating on an elegant shape, minimal decoration other than wood grain and a bold, curving line.

60. An American Chippendale Dining Table, c1770

Probably from Philadelphia, this table was made during that city's time as the nation's capital and its prominence as the centre of Rococo-style furniture production in America. Thomas Affleck's arrival from London in 1763 boosted this first real flowering of American style, although many local craftsmen, such as William Savery, Jonathan Shoemaker and Benjamin Randolph, were also working in the same vein.

Philadelphia had a tradition of generously proportioned furniture, seen here in the beautiful long, curving drop leaves, emphasized by the arch in the apron at the end, and the bold, curving cabriole legs, which end in magnificent ball-and-claw feet. The table shows a new angularity after the preceding Queen Anne style, reflecting the confidence of Philadelphia's cabinetmakers.

60

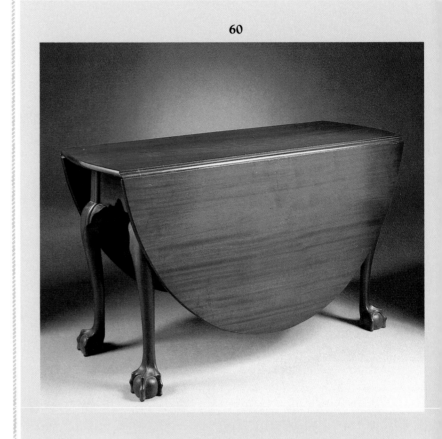

62

61

59

61. An American Chippendale Card Table, Rhode Island, c1765

This mahogany card table is probably by John Goddard (1723–85) of Newport, Rhode Island. It is a good example of the transition between American Queen Anne and American Chippendale taste. Queen Anne is associated with plainer forms, flat, undecorated surfaces, and simplicity, as seen here on the top and apron. The shell decoration which characterized this Queen Anne-influenced local form can be seen on the front cabriole leg of this card table. American Chippendale looks more to English Rococo – cabriole legs, ball-and-claw feet, decoration and outlines with tight curves. All of these influences could have been found in Thomas Chippendale's *Director,* known to have been available in America during the 1760s.

Such pieces were usually of carved (but rarely inlaid) mahogany, and the carcasses were sometimes made of secondary woods – a clue to the main furniture-making centres. Philadelphia, then the nation's capital, was famous for its cabinetmakers, Thomas Affleck, William Savery, Jonathan Shoemaker and Benjamin Randolph, all of whose Rococo furniture rivalled the best of European work. Newport and Boston created Chippendale furniture with its own distinctive style, adhering to a linear tradition and a tending toward tall, thin proportions.

John Goddard was one of over 20 members of the Goddard and Townsend furniture-making dynasty, interrelated Quaker families which dominated the trade between 1760 and 1780.

62. A Pair of George III Satinwood Card Tables, c1775

Designed to sit against a wall, this pair of *demi-lune* (half-moon) card tables have a less obvious function – card tables when in use, they were also intended to fill wall space between the numerous windows in Georgian houses. This use is similar to that of pier tables (so-named after the architectural term 'pier', which refers to the supporting wall between two windows), although these were sometimes more elaborate and generally shallower than card tables, so they protruded less from the wall.

Satinwood, which was lighter and less sombre than mahogany, was a favourite with the Georgians. The bands of foliate inlay on a mahogany background which edge the table tops are heightened by the use of harewood, a sycamore veneer stained grey-green. Although the table aprons are plain, the decoration at the top of each leg uses the oval motif which was so fundamental to Georgian design.

45

63. A George III Sycamore and Gilt Gesso Side Table, *c*1775

Robert Adam (1728–1792) and his contemporaries in the mid 18th century were to have a profound effect on the history of furniture. Adam himself was a real innovator, often producing furniture with no precedent whatsoever; inevitably, some of his experiments were more successful than others. When considering furniture of this period, it must be remembered that much was designed for a specific setting, providing an essential background for the piece.

This style of table, for example, never became popular. The combination of an all-wood top on a gilt gesso base feels slightly wrong (the top would look better with tapering legs, the base with a marble top). The textured frieze decoration, too, clashes with the finely grained sycamore top, showing neo-Classical motifs of a central vase form and scrolling leaves on a background of satinwood. Perhaps if restored to its original brilliant gilt state and put in a sympathetic setting, the table could be seen in a different, more positive light.

64. An English George III Mahogany Serving or Side Table, *c*1775

A handsome and functional piece of furniture, this 5ft (1.52m) wide table would have stood at the side of a room and been used for serving. Its serpentine front in a bow shape tempers its rectangular form, and was a feature of English design of the 1770s and 1780s. The two frieze drawers with handles follow the same line.

As a concession to the elaborate carved furniture of the 1760s, there are small, carved oval decorations above the table's stout but tapering legs; these are echoed at the top of the legs themselves. This transitional period in design was beginning to anticipate the change during the 1780s and 1790s from three-dimensional (carved) ornamentation to flatter surfaces with applied decoration in the form of paint, lacquer or inlay.

The slightly heavy proportions and stout block feet of this table suggest that it might be Irish, but furniture was produced on such a grand scale, and generally from pattern books, that it is hard to be certain of its origin. Pattern-book drawings had a tremendous influence on design, the most renowned among them being Thomas Chippendale's *The Gentleman and Cabinet-maker's Director*, which was published in three editions between 1754 and 1762.

63

65. An English George III Mahogany Architect's or Drawing Table, c1780

This elegant and restrained work table is typically English, reflecting both the Georgian fascination with mechanical furniture (as seen in contemporary exercise chairs and bureaux with discreet drawers in their base) and the aspirations of the Georgian Renaissance man.

The simplest of a series of writing tables, it has two ratchets which allow the working surface to lie completely flat, like a desk, or to be set at any angle required. The understatement in the design is particularly clear in the tapering legs and the drawers – the latter have no handles, and are only distinguishable by the cock-beaded outlines.

Educated Georgians were often concerned with the planning of their own properties (Lord Burlington, for example, was largely responsible for the design of Chiswick House, London, in the mid 18th century) and architectural tables date from this time, a concrete reminder of Georgian interests.

1700-1800

66. A Louis XVI Marquetry Table by Charles Topino, *c*1780

This beautiful chest of drawers was made by Charles Topino (1742–1803), who specialized in very high-quality pieces of small furniture. It has three drawers which are disguised by the superb marquetry decoration; the top and front have landscape panels, the sides are decorated with garlands and foliage, including typical neo-classical motifs such as sheaves of wheat and flowers. The discreet lines of the furniture are slightly negated by the effusive decoration and colour.

Although originally successful, Topino, like many cabinetmakers, suffered at the hands of the French Revolution and was declared bankrupt in 1789.

67. A Louis XVI Gilt Wood Console Table, *c*1780

In design history, the Louis XVI period saw a considerable exchange of ideas and craftsmen between England and France. This piece is very similar to many console tables used by Robert Adam in his interiors for the English aristocracy during the 1770s and 1780s. The French *ébéniste* (cabinetmaker) Georges Jacob was known to be working for the English Royal Family over the last part of the century, and pieces of his from this date can still be seen at Windsor Castle, near London.

The table has a half-moon top and fluted legs, and its frieze is heightened by a *guilloche* and egg-and-tongue decoration, architectural forms and motifs favoured by the English. But there are signs of its French origin: the legs seem stouter for the frieze than would usually be seen in England, and the stretcher is heavy. Both features give the table a more solid appearance which is quite antithetical to the spirit of Adam's designs.

68. A French Iron *Guéridon, c*1780

This piece is difficult to date accurately, but the curved legs suggest a possible date of *c*1760. It is close to the *guéridon's* original function as a candlestand, with a narrow top designed to hold candelabra and an adjustable shaft which allowed the height of the light source to vary.

The contemporary English craftsman, Matthew Boulton (1728–1809), produced similar pieces in his workshops in London and Birmingham, although these tended to be in gilt bronze of very high quality, following the French lead in ormolu. This is virtually the only form of metal furniture found in England during this period, although some exotic silver furniture exists at Knole in Kent, made for Charles II.

69. A Louis XVI Steel *Guéridon, c*1780

This most unusual table follows the design of wood-tripod *guéridons*, which were generally more popular in England than in France. Its style, with gallery and marble top, is similar to that of Louis XVI, but it is difficult to be sure of its date without documents.

Even though the French had a continuous tradition of metalworking from the Middle Ages onward, the finely turned steel stem on spindling, curving tripod legs had little precedent, and seems contemporary enough to have come from the 20th century, perhaps the Art Deco period of Bauhaus school.

70. An English George III Sycamore Pembroke Table, *c*1780

This delicate table embodies the height of Hepplewhite or Sheraton ideals of decoration. Made of sycamore, which itself has a shimmering grain, the table is cross-banded in tulipwood. The detail illustrates nearly the entire Georgian vocabulary of decoration: a large shell-shaped inlay is framed by an anthemion and urn-draped foliate scrolls; this in turn is surrounded by portrait medallions, hung from ribbons and joined by swags of husks. The tapering legs on castors are also classically Georgian, and the table has a single drawer in the frieze.

According to Thomas Sheraton, Pembroke tables take their name from 'that lady who first gave orders for one of them, who probably gave the first idea of such a table to the workmen'. Introduced during the 1750s, they have two flaps supported by hinge brackets and were originally rectangular, although later pieces are more often oval or have serpentine edges. Pembroke tables are essentially practical items, as can be seen from Adam's designs; wherein console and side tables were clearly for decoration but Pembroke tables such as this one were in constant domestic use.

66

68

70

67

69

71. An English George III Mahogany Envelope Games Table, c1780

This rare envelope card table is far more unusual than other *demi-lune,* D-shaped or serpentine-fronted games tables of the period, and is particularly distinguished for bearing the name of its maker – C Toussaint. Although it is certainly an English-made piece, the maker's French name implies that he might have been one of a number of French craftsmen who went to England during the 18th century to learn the trade at a time when English fashions were very popular in France.

The table is typically George III, with its squareness, straight lines and tapering legs. The cross-banded pattern in satinwood and tulipwood on the top is very much of the period, as is the circular decoration in boxwood radiating from the centre. As expected in a card table, the leaves fold out to increase the size of the playing area, but it is very unusual for the closed leaves to form the pattern of an envelope.

The table is photographed here to show it both open and closed, and it can be seen that its playing area is bare wood. As most card tables are thought of as being baize-lined (although there are exceptions to the rule), it is possible that this might have been designed as an occasional or tea table.

72. An English George III Satinwood Hepplewhite Dressing Table, c1780

From the front, this table appears to be a small commode (chest of drawers), with a drawer which pulls out and a sliding flap to the side which extends to hold the paraphernalia of dressing and make-up. In fact, the front is a dummy drawer, and the hinged lid, decorated with the typical neo-classical decoration of an urn surrounded by scrolls, lifts upward to reveal a fitted interior.

The pronounced serpentine edge of the table top and the elegant cabriole legs veneered in cross grain both owe a debt to French design of the time. This was a period when many ideas were exchanged across the English Channel, and in fact this style is sometimes known as 'French Hepplewhite'. Both Sheraton and Hepplewhite included a range of similar tables in their pattern-books, many of which included Georgian gadgetry such as roll tops or full-length ratcheted mirrors.

The stylishness of the piece could well be due to a habit women had at this time of receiving guests while dressing – thus requiring a dressing table that was both decorative and functional.

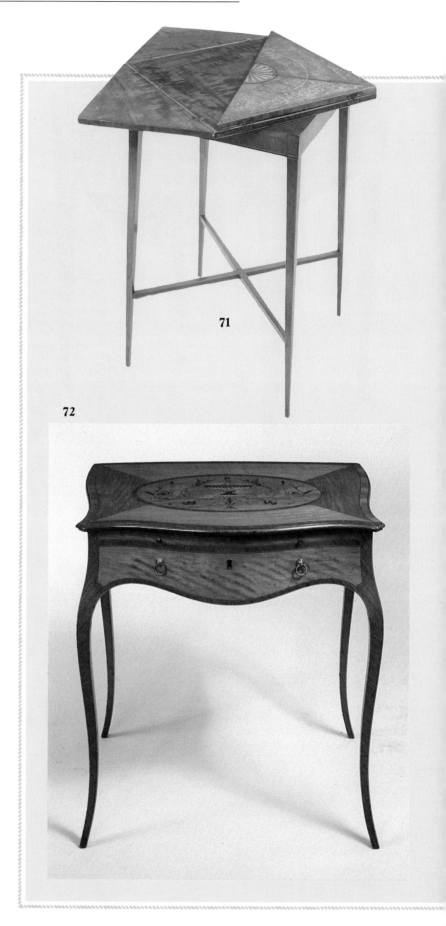

71

72

73

74

73. An English Hepplewhite Pembroke Table, *c*1785

Although the history of this table is unknown, there is a documented card table which shares many of the same characteristics. If, as is likely, the two were supplied together, they would have come from a leading cabinetmaker of the Hepplewhite era.

Three unusual features which the tables share are the dappled mahogany grain of the veneer (mahogany contours are usually broad); the geometric loops of the drawer handles, which have chamfered corners where the washers meet the wood; and the contrast of flat, two-dimensional figuring and crisp carving, seen here on the legs.

The table also has striking folding leaves with instepped quadrant corners. Its shape, which falls between circular and rectangular, is unusual. A superb example of a Pembroke table, this piece shows the refinement that was possible on even the most standard of table designs.

74. An English George III Satinwood Painted Card Table, *c*1785

The second half of George III's reign is sometimes known as 'The Age of Satinwood' and is considered by many to be the finest period of English decorated furniture. This beautifully executed table, probably one of a pair or even from a set of four, would have been very expensive even in its own time.

The table is covered in all types of Georgian painted decoration, including the centre panel, filled with musical trophies (instruments displayed artistically); the frame of floral garlands and ribbons, and the cross-banded edges of tulipwood and burr yew wood. The legs and sides are painted with similar motifs.

D-shaped, this piece follows the classic format for a card table of this date: a rear leg, hinged in the middle of the table back, swings out like a gate to support the top, which when unfolded reveals a baize-lined interior. A decade earlier the *demi-lune* (or half-moon) table was preferred, but by 1785 the D-shaped table had increased in popularity.

75. A Pair of English George III Caskets on Stands, *c*1785

The late Georgian period was one of considerable experimentation in design, exploring gadgetry and placing a variety of furniture on stands. The closed casket here is a work box, with room for needles, material, cottons, etc, and the open box is a teapoy, or tea caddy. This has two compartments on each side for different flavours (of mainly china teas), and two canisters which often still bear the labels 'Green' and 'Bohea', the two main varieties of the day. Tea was a very expensive commodity and was therefore locked away. A box like this also contained a blue glass bowl for the ritual of blending tea.

Both caskets have hinged lids and are decorated with cut-steel clasps. Some of these frame medallions were made by Matthew Boulton (1728–1809), who was best known for his silver and ormolu workshops and who specialized in metalwork.

76. A Marquetry Table by David Roentgen, *c*1785

David Roentgen (1743–1807) was the son of Abraham Roentgen, the renowned Saxon cabinetmaker who retired from his workshops at Neuwied on the Rhine in 1772. He was succeeded by David, who became Germany's most famous cabinetmaker of the time and was hugely successful, with established markets for his work in Berlin, Vienna and Paris. He became a *maître ébéniste* in France in 1780 and subsequently adopted the stamp 'DAVID'. His fame rested mainly on his inlay marquetry techniques – he created shadows by using different shades of wood, so that his finished work resembled mosaic. Previously, cabinetmakers had either engraved or burnt shadows into their pictures.

This simple oval table with disguised drawers is typical of his work. He collaborated with Pierre Kintzing, a famous mechanical toy and clockmaker, and specialized in hidden drawers such as these. In this case, one long drawer reveals four hidden ones when a secret catch is opened at the end of the table. Although the shape is clear, the inlay and colour on the top and sides detract from the simplicity of line, a typical pitfall when German craftsmen attempted neo-classical pieces such as this, perhaps because of the still-strong influence of the Rococo in Germany.

77. A Louis XVI *Table en Chiffonière*, *c*1785

The *table en chiffonière* is generally thought of as a small case of drawers on legs, sometimes with a writing slide. It is related to the *chiffonier*, a tall chest of drawers made in large numbers in the middle of the 18th century.

Straight-edged, this example has a pierced brass gallery, a marble top, and sides and drawers veneered in tulipwood and kingwood. Its only decoration is the ormolu surrounding the escutcheons and capping the feet. The bottom halves of the legs are the only curving lines on the entire piece.

In England, Thomas Chippendale noted the supply of 'a neat shiffener writing table, japanned in green and gold with a drawer and cut bottles' in his accounts in the 1760s, the first such reference to this French source.

78. A Louis XVI Inlaid Writing Table, *c*1785

The second half of the 18th century witnessed a trend throughout Europe toward smaller, more intimate rooms, which required appropriate furniture. Many small tables were made to meet this need, often less than 3ft (91cm) long. This table has two clear indications of its approximate date: the frieze has a *guilloche*, a gilded bronze band which is directly associated with neo-classical architectural ornament; and it is relatively plain for Louis XVI, and could therefore have been made after the Revolution in the 1790s.

It does, however, show typical Louis XVI elements. The leather writing surface in the centre of the top is plain, but is surrounded by a sophisticated band of interlacing marquetry of tulipwood and kingwood. The frieze is decorated with ormolu, and the legs, cross-banded and bordered in a darker wood, finish in neat brass caps.

75

78

77

76

1700-1800

79. A Louis XVI *Table à Ouvrage,* c1785

This piece is in the full-blown Louis XVI style. The characteristic brass gallery around the top of and undertier gives the table horizontal emphasis, contributing to the effect of straight lines and solidity which was typical of this time. The stretcher or tier here is used decoratively, to balance the weight of the box on top, and it functions as a shelf as well.

It is a sewing table, and the side flap folds down to reveal a fitted storage space with room for sewing equipment and materials. The marquetry decoration on the side is realistic, and in contrast to earlier tables has a clearly bordered, neat, floral pattern. The restraining border helps to give the table a more subdued feel than that of earlier, similar Rococo work boxes, in effect holding the design 'still'.

80. A Pair of Small French Console Tables by Georges Jacob, c1785

These small cupboard tables are typical of the contemporary passion for small furniture and for things English. *Anglomanie,* or Anglomania, was at its height during the 1780s, and these tables are basically French Chippendale; it is the brass gallery and marble top of these console tables which indicate that they are not actually English.

The carving is probably by Georges Jacob (1739–1814), the foremost carver of the period who worked in plain, gilt and painted woods. He was the founder of a line of cabinetmakers which included two sons, the younger of whom changed his name to Jacob-Desmalter and carried on the family business into the early 19th century. Born the son of a peasant in Burgundy, Jacob was a favourite of Marie-Antoinette's and reached his peak at the time of the Revolution. His closeness to the royal family meant that he was denounced several times during the Revolution, this despite his attempts to gain credibility, which included making gun stocks for the Revolutionary army. He died in a hospital asylum.

81. A Louis XV *Guéridon, c1785*

Although correct in all its individual elements, this piece somehow manages to give the impression of being assembled. The general elegance of the period is missing, and the *guéridon* features too many decorative ideas – none of which sets the tone for the whole table.

Almost all the elements were standard in the 1780s – the brass gallery, the heavy ormolu mounts around the drawers, the curved apron under each tier and the cross-

81

80

79

82

83

banding and marquetry inlay. So too were the curious outward-bowing supports above the cabriole legs, although if straight supports had been used, the whole table would have a much cleaner outline.

82. An American Federal Candlestand, c1785

This table was made specifically to hold candelabra or candlesticks and has a small drawer below to accommodate lighting equipment such as a tinder box and wax tapers. The candlestand dates from around 1785, which was technically the 'Federal' period following American independence in 1783. New styles being developed in England by Robert Adam were slow to arrive in America due to the war, and so are not reflected here.

The Queen Anne style was still being produced in America up to this time, and neo-classical furniture was fully absorbed in American style a decade or so later. This period is confusing because so many styles were made at the same time; country makers tended to be conservative.

This elegant table was probably made in Connecticut, and is of beautiful red cherry wood with an even grain. The beginnings of neo-classical influence can be seen here in the fan-shaped inlay on the top, the urn-like column, and the graceful angular tripod with small feet which are known as pointed snake feet.

83. An American Chippendale Card Table, c1790

The general construction of this table is closely based on a model popular from the 1770s and 1780s in England. The top hinges backward and the rear gate leg swings out to support it; the top edge has a chequered, key-fret moulding; the frieze above the legs has a cross-hatched edge; and the fluted, tapering legs end in Marlboro feet.

While the table is made up of English elements in an English construction, the decorative motifs are combined in such a way as to make this table very American. The frieze decoration is not a true classical motif, and the legs are fluted in a solid manner slightly out of keeping with the table top.

Probably from Connecticut or Rhode Island, it is made of cherry wood, in keeping with the Americans' extensive use of fruitwoods, and is from the transitional time between the Chippendale and Federal periods – the former associated with carving and decoration, the latter with neo-classicism and architectural detail.

84. A Russian Oval Table, *c1790*

The inspiration behind this table is clearly the French neo-classical style of the 1780s. Much Russian furniture followed designs from Western Europe, although they were often imbued with a regional flavour. In this case, for instance, the top of finely figured mahogany, the extensive use of linear ormolu decoration and the unusual stretcher are all Russian additions, although the basic shape of the table, the pierced gallery and the details on the legs are standard neo-classical features.

Similar examples to this are to be found in the Pavlovsk Palace near Leningrad, and several inventories from before the Russian Revolution of 1917 include many French pieces of this date.

85. An English George III Mahogany Pembroke Table, *c1790*

This standard round-top Georgian Pembroke table is the more desirable of the two main models, ie, round – and rectangular-topped. A good early example, the table is circular when the flaps are extended, and has tapering legs. Later Regency and Victorian Pembroke tables often have turned legs, and use a lesser mahogany than the well-figured wood here.

Tulipwood – a striped wood from Brazil used almost exclusively for banding – was a favourite with the Georgians, and is used here in the cross-banding around the table edge. Satinwood too is used, a contrast with the dominant darker mahogany. Other classic Georgian decorative motifs can be seen in the oval inlaid panel at the top of the legs, which terminate in brass capping and castors.

86. An English George III Mahogany Architect's Table, *c1790*

This practical architect's table has a sophisticated double ratchet with an unusual mechanism. It also contains a frieze drawer that is divided into compartments for inks, paper, etc, and two drop-leaf wings on each side which can be extended to increase the working surface.

Nicely detailed, with castors for moving the table around the room and a ledge on the work surface to support the drawings, this piece is made from classic Georgian flame mahogany, so-called after the enormous contours of the wood which result in a flame pattern.

88

86

87

85

84

89

87. An English George III Mahogany Artist's Table, c1790

This elegant baize-lined table has a lighter frame than most other architect's tables. It also has a double-ratcheted mechanism which withdraws into a tailor-made mahogany cover, secured by a loop. When folded, the table covers an aperture to hold a palette, and the undertier is shaped to fit the knees of the artist.

Showing all the signs of a Georgian gadget, this adjustable artist's table is indicative of the contemporary vogue for sketching, watercolours and oil painting – 'during the 18th century such tables were seen as very healthy for those who stand to read, write or draw'; *The Dictionary of English Furniture* (1st Edition) captioned a similar table from the Noel Terry Collection in York, England. The same type of table was used by the Reverend Edward Hoyle, who stands reading at one in a 1760 painting by the renowned English portrait painter, Arthur Devis.

88. An American Federal Pembroke Table, c1790

This sombre, utilitarian Pembroke table is made of mahogany. It follows the English patterns popular at this date, and is probably by John Townsend (1732–1809) of Newport, Rhode Island. Much influenced by Chippendale, he came from one of the important Quaker cabinetmaking families of Newport, and is thought to have settled in Connecticut.

The construction and inlay decoration of this table are similar to other pieces by Townsend. Its severe rectangular look is relieved only by a little inlay at the ends, with 'book end' inlay (fluting) above the carrot – and line-inlaid legs with cross-banded cuffs (the small decoration at the end of the legs).

89. A Sheraton Mahogany Drum-topped Table, c1795

Understatement was an essential characteristic of Georgian design: the art lay in what was not stated. The success of this table, which is extremely simple, lies in its excellent proportions. The diameter of the top almost exactly matches the diameter of the splayed tripod legs (which are cleanly stopped with brass-capped castors), and no jagged edges, scrolls or carving break the severity of line. In fact, there is very little decoration at all, apart from the natural grain of the wood and the neat ivory escutcheons around the keyholes.

90. An English George III Triple Pedestal Mahogany Dining Table, c1795

The extendable English dining table went back to the middle of the 17th century, when there was a change in style from large, static oak tables placed in the great hall to mobile, lighter furniture. Woods such as walnut and oak, used in the 17th century, were increasingly replaced by mahogany for almost all dining tables after 1720, when import tax on colonial woods were lifted.

The pedestal dining table, such as this example, belonged to the second half of the 18th century, and had the advantage of being infinitely extendable. At Hardwick Hall in Derbyshire, for example, there is a dining table with five four-legged pedestals supporting it on turned reeded columns. It is rare nowadays to find tables with more than two pedestals; the leaves and pedestals of such tables are often replaced, broken into small arrangements and reassembled with different veneers. These tables can be almost entirely dismantled, as the pedestal fits into a block on the underside of the leaves, usually with removable brass bolts.

This example has all the essential late Georgian characteristics: strong, red-coloured top with matching veneer; turned columns on the pedestals; elegant sabre legs; and brass claw castors. The style continued into the 19th century, albeit in a more angular form.

Georgian design was much occupied with construction and proportion.

91. An English George III Library Drum Table, c1795

In the early 18th century, library tables intended as decorative furniture became more specialized. They were large, grand and stood in the centre of the room, often without drawers. This more practical example, however, has a tooled-leather surface for writing and eight drawers – an impressive piece of cabinetmaking, as four of these are rectangular, the other four triangular. Much smaller than early 18th-century examples, the table swivels on its central turned support and rests on three splayed legs. This circular form is known as a drum table because of its shape.

92. A French Porcelain and Ormolu *Guéridon, c1795*

Small round tables such as these were popular in France at the end of the 18th century and during the Empire period of the early 19th century. They were both functional and of very high quality, often using porcelain plaques decorated individually by known artists. The Impressionist painter, Pierre-Auguste Renoir, for example, painted porcelain plates during the mid 19th century to make a living.

In this case, the central plaque shows French 18th-century porcelain at its best, decorated with breathtaking realism. It is supported by a finely wrought ormolu base, with the legs pared down to simulate bamboo and a slender three-pronged stretcher which would be hard to reproduce in wood. The table is in the style of Adam Weisweiler (c1750–c1810), who probably trained with David Roentgen before moving in the 1770s to Paris, where he worked until around 1810.

93. An English George III Pembroke Table, c1795

This stunning and refined Pembroke table clearly demonstrates the meeting of two eras in furniture design, that of the Georgian 'Age of Satinwood' (1770–1800) and the Regency 'Age of Rosewood' which immediately followed. This serpentine-edged table has a centre of dark rosewood surrounded by an apron of bright satinwood, the two slightly separated by tulipwood cross-banding.

Difficult to date precisely, the table's small oval fan inlays are a classic George III motif, which implies a time around the turn of the century, and the table shows a concern with style typical of Georgian furniture. Many specialists claim that the late Georgian/early Regency period represented the peak of English craftsmanship and design; pieces such as this are at the height of late Georgian taste.

94. An English Late George III Card Table, c1795

This attractive serpentine-fronted card table with inward-curving sides opens out into an elegant star shape. Confusingly, it has a combination of different decorative styles: the loop swags on the frieze in boxwood inlay are reminiscent of the 1780s; the star inlay and fluted legs are both typical Regency figures; and the elegant tapering legs are slightly sculptural, a feature normally associated with the very early 19th century. Nevertheless, the overall shape of the piece is appealing, and it is topped with well-figured mahogany.

92

90

91

93

94

1800 TO 1900

This early 19th-century interior shows typical Biedermeier furniture. The 'bois clairs' (pale woods) used c1830 show the reaction against the heavy-looking mahogany used during the first Empire until 1815, which often appeared with elaborate gilt bronze mounts. Here decoration such as carving or painting is minimal, and the plain surfaces and straight edges give a sombre, even ponderous air, unlike extrovert 18th century furniture. This is the beginning of the look which came to be Victorian: at best an uncluttered showing of native woods by contrasting colours and textures.

Tables in the 18th century began with the likes of Italian Baroque extravagances featuring marble tops and gilt scrolling supports, and ended with severe, neo-Classical examples from England, with plain mahogany veneers, straight legs and tempered further with stark, geometric outlines. France, so long at the forefront of furniture fashion, also produced more restrained tables toward 1790, although their surfaces still bore exotic veneers with rich gilt-bronze mounts. The French Revolution severed not only royal heads but also orders for very opulent and expensive tables. All these factors should have led to the year 1800 opening with the production of humble and unassuming, dark and sober furnishing. On the contrary, the opposite occurred.

At the outset of the 19th century, furniture designers were receiving their inspiration from two significant sources: forms and decoration newly imported from Egypt and the Middle East as a result of the Napoleonic wars there; and the same of Greece, due to recent excavations there (formerly only Roman ruins had been known). In addition, when the French royal furniture made before the Revolution was auctioned, literally millions of exotic pieces were sold cheaply all over Europe, which prompted a wide-ranging taste for imaginative work based on these elaborate, well-made 'prototypes'. Hybrid tables appeared in full force, sporting the likes of sphinx legs, massive hairy-paw feet and scrolling frieze decorations reminiscent of Arabic writing. In general, the output of this period was on a grand scale fitting for the emperor Napoleon's imperial interiors – and those of his relatives – throughout Europe.

England, the other furniture fashion leader, especially influenced designers in North America, where 18th-century furniture had followed George III style; Federal tables made after the War of Independence in 1782 followed Chippendale's pattern-books, with carving and scrolls, and then those of Hepplewhite and Sheraton, whose conservative Georgian tables, with their severe, geometric elements, continued to be popular into the 19th century.

England in the early 1800s produced Regency furniture, sometimes known as 'English Empire'; the tables were as equally exotic as earlier Gallic Régence examples, and were adorned with animal heads and feet and bright wood grains such as black and yellow striped calamander wood from the West Indies. Ivory inlay and veneer were popular on tables, and brass stringing and inlay often brightened plain woods. Thomas Hope (1769–1831) produced a pattern-book comprising furniture designs from his own home, all of which were sympathetic to his famed antiquities collection – and proved highly popular with British cabinet-makers. The taste gradually reached across the Atlantic, where Duncan Phyfe (1768–1854) began to dominate New York cabinet-making, supplying a rapidly expanding market with good-quality, mostly mahogany furniture; these assumed ever more sculptural shapes, for example, carved animal feet which continued on some tables well up to the tops of the legs.

The brilliance of the Empire period shone – and was celebrated – into the 1820s. Tables especially honoured the martial arts, with sabre legs curving outward like military swords, aprons studded with gilt stars on dramatically dark backgrounds akin to smart uniforms, and stretchers carved in rope-twist forms recalling the sea victories of Nelson.

The second quarter of the century, however, saw a return to relative mediocrity. After the fall of Napoleon, the homely Biedermeier style became popular on the Continent, chiefly in Germany and Austria. No-nonsense tables using native woods such as birch and ash appeared, undecorated on the tops and around the deep aprons. Known as *bois clairs*, the woods seemed dull compared with Empire veneers. Much Biedermeier furniture was usually quite massive, producing a ponderous effect, although good examples of tables were made throughout Europe (including Scandinavia and Russia), which were simple yet elegant and nicely functional. Many Biedermeier tables are similar to plainer versions of English Regency tables.

At this time English designs became rather heavy, with dark, dull tops of every possible shape above deep aprons on thick, scrolling legs; in other words, tables thought of as typically Victorian. The 1840s and 1850s were also a period of revivals. Gilt Rococo tables appeared, as did neo-Gothic tables with arches and carved legs, and Tudor Revival oak refectory tables. Somewhat ironically, many of these historicizing designs were of better quality than the originals, mostly due to their having the Victorian advantage of new technologies and high-powered machines. Some of the tables illustrated in this section were included in the catalogue of the 1851 Crystal Palace Exhibition, an international trade fair held in London which presented a cross-section of tables: traditional, revival and innovative. Among the latter, papier mâché was a popular new material. Likewise, table legs took on exciting new looks – from Thonet's bent-rosewood examples in Austria to American models featuring cast iron and unusual native-wood supports.

After the mid-century loss of direction, table design branched into the revivalist Arts & Crafts Movement, whose primary exponents were critic John Ruskin (1819–1900) and multi-talented designer/writer William Morris (1834–1896). Furniture workshops were set up which, according to the guidelines of Morris et al, ignored mechanization and modern factory methods and instead looked back idealistically to the medieval past.

Some furniture makers attempted to return to a village-based craftsman system, whereby an individual fashioned an entire piece of furniture, this often designed by a notable artist of the time, such as the Pre-Raphaelite painter, Dante Gabriel Rossetti. The results of this working method were various – at best, tables of exotic shapes and distant inspiration were made in the Japanese style, including lacquerwork, or some copied Arabic designs with Moorish motifs.

In terms of shape and decoration, some Arts & Crafts tables overlapped with country furniture, which continued to coexist – as always – alongside the expensive pieces of furniture made for wealthy, discerning clients. These more rustic tables. such as those made by the so-called Cotswold school, were usually of excellent quality and classic design, but at times they could be mediocre models characterized not by a Georgian simplicity but by heavy stretchers and tops. The folk tradition is perhaps best shown by the works of the Shakers and other retrospective communities and groups in the United States who, rather than attempting to copy the past, simply continued the use of their ancestors' traditional skills and forms.

The Arts & Crafts Movement is significant for two reasons. First, it embodied the re-examination of style which gave tables a self-conscious look and, secondly, it paved the way for the rectilinear arm of *fin-de-siècle* style, which combined art and innovation to create distinctive tables and other items of furniture. Morris's and others' new way of looking at and making everyday objects was to have its effect c1900 on designers and craftsmen in areas as scattered as Glasgow, Vienna and Chicago.

95. A Portuguese Card Table, *c*1800

It is the tortoiseshell veneer that gives this piece its striking appearance, although structurally it is a standard D-shaped card table. Portuguese colonies in the West Indies and Central America allowed the indulgence of a taste for exotic veneer, and it is fairly common to come across 18th-century furniture and precious cabinets treated in this way.

Tortoiseshell decoration took two main forms. The first used clear shell through which colour from the wood could be viewed, and the second, seen here, employed various shades of the shell – blond (light) and dark – for contrast. In fact, the fan inlay on the table top and the panels around the frieze are reminiscent of Northern European satinwood and mahogany equivalents, but tortoiseshell pieces are far rarer.

96. A French Directoire Mahogany *Tric-trac* Table, *c*1800

The lid of this mahogany games table lifts off to reveal a sunken backgammon board, and its drawers would have contained the pieces required for playing. The game *tric-trac* was an early form of backgammon and was played all over Europe (in England it was known as 'trick-track'); its name derives from the sound of pieces hitting the board.

A typical piece of Directoire furniture – so-called after the post-Revolution French government of 1795–99, and referring to late 18th- and very early 19th-century furniture – it shows clear George III Regency influences in its fluted legs, echoed on the corners of the table itself. The carved decoration and gilded brass details help to lighten the piece somewhat.

97. An English Regency Games Table, *c*1800

This versatile games table with concealed chess-board top, sliding flap for candlesticks and a drawer which turns into a writing surface with inkwell and pen tray shows all the signs of Georgian preoccupation with gadgetry. Small, well-proportioned and neat, it was probably for occasional use, and may once have had a well for sewing. The piece's straight lines indicate influence from the late George III period, as typified by Sheraton and Hepplewhite. The use of rosewood on the top and the turned stretchers that are both round- and square-sectioned give it a Regency flavour.

97

95

96

98. An English Library or Writing Table, *c*1800

This curious table seems unusually proportioned, and on closer inspection it is clear that its legs have been cut down, perhaps due to damage. This leaves an impression of a low and very wide table, and the eight legs give it a feeling of grandeur. It has drawers on both its sides and ends – although those on the ends are dummies – and the small centre frieze drawer is fitted with compartments for writing equipment. The drawer outlines and line decoration may seem slightly unrealistic and excessive, but may well have been added at a later date; it was quite common for changes in taste to lead to a change in veneer in this way.

99. A French Empire *Guéridon*, *c*1800

This *guéridon*, with its small circular top, clearly performs the same function of the original *guéridon* – that of candlestand. It shows traces of the Louis XVI style, ie, the marble top with brass gallery, which sits on a straight neo-classical central column ending in three hipped cabriole feet. Overall, it is severe, the only decoration being a bit of ormolu. As such, it reflects the attitude of Republican France (at which time it was made), whose people were trying to emulate Roman nobility in terms of furniture making, as well as other arts.

100. An American Federal Dining Table, *c*1805

This remarkable table is nearly 17ft (5.2m) long and 5ft (1.5m) wide. It has two end sections with leaves above a cock-beaded frieze, tripods at the ends and three double scrolled supports. These end in brass animal paw feet and castors. The six mahogany and four poplar leaves are an unusual combination, based on a patent by Gillow's of London and Lancaster, and referred to today as having an accordion action.

In the United States, this type of mechanism was mostly used in New York, although this table was made in Philadelphia and was supposedly the property of Thomas Jefferson, President of the United States from 1801 to 1809. Jefferson spent some time in Europe, and his Virginia house, Monticello, which he personally designed along the lines of Italian-revival architectural principles, contained much European, or American European, furniture. This table was given to the Maryland Historical Society in 1924.

102

100

101

98

99

101. A Regency English Calamander Sofa Table, *c*1805

The most striking feature of this stunning sofa table is its unusual wood. Calamander was imported from Ceylon and has contrasting patterns (brown, mottled and streaked) of dark brown or black on a paler background. A fine-grained hardwood, it became popular for veneering and cross-banding over a period of 50 years or so from 1780.

The wood is strongly associated with the Regency period and the table shows many other classic Regency features. The brass strung border to the table top is studded with stars (known as a stella border), and the legs are also brass strung, with brass cappings cast with a leafy decoration. This table amply demonstrates the Regency interest in a variety of patterns, in contrasting colours and in brass inlay.

Sofa tables were made to accompany sofas, and not settees. Settees generally had a hardwood (often mahogany) frame and were designed for halls. On the whole, they were less comfortable and certainly less fashionable than Regency sofas, which were lavishly upholstered and typically accompanied by a matching table.

102. An American Federal Work Table, *c*1805

It is likely that this carved mahogany work table is by Duncan Phyfe (1768–1854), or from his New York workshop. The beginnings of the style for heavy carving that arrived in the early 19th century can clearly be seen here.

The top part of the round section is plain, with finely figured veneer, but the bottom half shows a reeded 'tambour' (sliding door) made of vertical slats which slide into the side panels. The amount of texture indicates that the style for plain wood has gone, and the deep top section gives the table a heavier feel. The elegant, sweeping legs are both reeded and carved.

105

104

103. An American Federal Dressing Bureau, c1805

This American dressing table was probably made by John and Thomas Seymour of Boston, Massachusetts, and is clearly influenced by European Sheraton furniture. Light and elegant, it has square, tapering legs and contrasting inlay of mahogany and bird's-eye maple. The long, shallow drawers emphasize the horizontal feel, and the elongated mirror is supported by curving brackets – the only part of the piece which is not a straight line.

The term 'Federal' refers to furniture made towards the end of the 18th century and the beginning of the 19th, broadly corresponding to English late Georgian or Regency taste. As with many other American designs, basic English styles were adapted with regional variations.

John Seymour (c1738–1818) was a major figure in Massachusetts furniture circles. British born, he emigrated to America with his son, Thomas, arriving in Maine in 1785 and settling in Boston in 1794. They worked for a wealthy clientele, producing high-quality work – contrasting woods were one of their specialities, and their output was much influenced by Thomas Sheraton and George Hepplewhite.

104. An American Federal Dining Table, c1805

This table has a hinged section in the middle which can be used as a separate table. The two serpentine-ended external tables can also double as sideboards. With the intermediate flaps, the whole table stretches to amost 14ft (1.7m) in length.

It was probably made in the workshop of Duncan Phyfe (1768–1854), the best-known and probably most influential New York Federal cabinetmaker. His work related closely to that of the English Regency style. Phyfe's family emigrated from Scotland to Albany, New York, in the 1780s. Young Phyfe then worked as a joiner in New York City, where he had a shop from 1795 to 1847. This sold a large number of his original variations on European styles, which often included references to Greek and Roman design and featured his strange animal feet which extended up the leg.

Before Independence, New York had been secondary in furniture making, but after 1780 it grew rapidly and soon had the largest group of cabinetmakers in the nation. Generally, Hepplewhite and Sheraton designs were followed, interpreted by makers such as Michael Allison and Elbert Anderson.

103

105. An Empire *Guéridon, c*1805

In its role as a small occasional table for domestic use, the *guéridon* reached its peak of popularity in the early 19th century. Essentially the same form as the earlier Louis XVI version, the decoration and style on this table are pure neo-classical.

The table is made of mahogany, a favourite wood of the Empire period, and one that was increasingly scarce; its shortage was due to the English blockade of French ports, thus raising its price and leading to an increased use of indigenous woods such as oak, elm, ash, maple and beech in France. The table's top is a plain grained granite surrounded by an ormolu rim, which had by this time taken the place of a gallery. The sabre-shaped supports end in a Greek key pattern (a classical motif very popular in the Napoleonic era) and sit on a concave tripod base. The tripod frieze itself has typical classical architectural panels.

During the Consulate and Empire periods in French history (1799–1804 and 1804–15, respectively), furniture production recommenced after the upheavals of the Revolution. Although less refined than during the eras of Louis XIV, XV and XVI, the industry still employed over 10,000 workers in more than 100 workshops. One leading manufacturer alone, Jacob-Desmalter, employed over 400 men and exported one-third of its output.

1800-1900

106. An English Regency Mahogany Serving Table, *c*1807

One of the most influential designers in the Regency taste (known formally as English Empire) was Dutch-born Thomas Hope (1769–1831); this monumental, chunky serving table of his stands at over 6ft (1.8m) wide. When not used for serving, it would have been decorated with silverware and ceramics of the time, including such objects as centrepieces and knife urns, which opened to reveal stands for cutlery.

The piece shows a clear departure from the prevailing George III furniture styles – generally thought to end around 1800 – and the influences of its dominant designers, Adam, Hepplewhite and Sheraton. Not light, flowered, nor detailed, the table reflects Hope's interest in the antiquities of Greece, Egypt and the Middle East, and, as with many of his works, is a combination of several styles, borrowing a leg here, a stone frieze there.

Hope himself was a friend of the French architect/designer, Charles Percier (1764–1838), renowned for his severity of style and his quote: 'I scarcely was able to hold a pencil when instead of flowers, landscapes and other familiar objects, I began dealing in those straight lines which seem so little attractive to the greatest number'. Often twinned with George Smith as a provider of avant-garde designs, Hope in fact, like Smith, was absorbing ideas which were current in Europe and presenting them in a coherent form.

107. A German Neo-Classical Writing Table, *c*1810

Traditional German furniture had a history of carved decoration and dark woods which stretched back to the 16th century. Court furniture, however, was largely influenced by French design, although several renowned cabinet-makers were at work, including the brothers David (1743–1807) and Abraham Roentgen (1711–93).

This desk is typical of early 19th-century neo-classical work throughout Europe, combining elements of English and French style from the end of the 18th century. The pierced brass gallery on both tiers is a classic Louis XVI feature, as are the ormolu appliqués. The overall shape of the desk is very similar to Regency writing desks, and the fluted legs seem to anticipate William IV style.

This type of furniture was also very popular in Austria. Vienna was the centre of the Austro-Hungarian Empire, and pieces such as this were used to furnish official state rooms such as those of the Wüzburg Residenz, refurbished by Johann Valentin Raab in the early 19th century.

108. A Regency Mahogany Writing Table, *c*1810

This small writing table is interesting for its unusual mechanism, which allows the table to be adjusted. When used as a writing desk, the central leather-tooled surface lies flat; when employed for reading or drawing, it can be tipped to the angle required.

The table stands on unusual twin trestle ends which finish in splayed sabre legs. The reeded decoration and panelling of the frieze drawers, which are fitted with compartments, are typical of the Regency period, as is the preoccupation with gadgetry.

109. A Regency Writing Table, *c*1810

At the end of the 1700s, before the Empire styles of the early 19th century, furniture design lost some of its nationalist tendencies (Louis XV, George III, etc) and became more international. This was an obvious product of a world with better communications, coming at a time when British design was very popular in mainland Europe, and French and Italian design was influential in England.

This table shows two contrasting influences, an English Regency severity of line, and a French Louis XVI passion for gilt mounts. The latter is seen also in the pierced brass gallery around the back of the table top, in the gilt beading of the drawers and legs, and in the central ormolu mask. However, the mixture of styles works well, and this functional table exhibits a fine balance of decoration and line.

107

108

109

106

110. An American Federal Carved Mahogany Work Table, *c*1810

This small, distinctive work table stands 29in (73.5cm) high and is probably the work of Henry Connelly, the Philadelphia cabinetmaker whose furniture is often associated with that of his contemporary, Ephraim Haines. It was bought from Henry Connelly by the great-grandmother of the present owner.

Although not beautiful, it is a striking piece, with highly original applied decoration on each corner which comes as a complete contrast to the finely carved column and quadruped base. The table was made during a period in American history when native styles began to depart drastically from European traditions; here, for instance, the base is very European, while the top is a product of the maker's imagination.

A city with a strong neo-classical tradition, Philadelphia boasted over 100 cabinetmakers at this time. The screw-thread decoration on the top is a version of the original idea of flanking classical columns, although the rather busy threads give a less tranquil effect.

111. A Federal Mahogany Card Table, *c*1810

This card table was probably made in New York. The plain faces of the top and geometric line show an interest in the quality of the veneer rather than the decoration, and give the table a similarity to the Biedermeier furniture of Europe between 1820 and 1840. The supports of this table are four slender carved columns with splayed feet, and overall the table is beautifully proportioned. The visual weight of the top is almost exactly equal to that of the base.

It is an original and elegant piece, and although unattributed, it was obviously made by a cabinetmaker of considerable distinction.

110

111

113

112

112. A French Empire Gilt Wood Console Table, c1810

The period after the French Revolution of 1793 saw a succession of short governments in France. These included the Directoire (1795–99), the Consulat (1799–1804) and the Empire (1804–15). All three are terms loosely applied to the characteristic furniture of their respective periods, but they all reject the typically ornate, gilt-encrusted French furniture styles of the 18th century.

Exotic influences, and particularly Egyptian ones, are most associated with the Empire period. After Napoleon I's victory at the Battle of the Pyramids in 1800, both the French and English plundered considerable amounts of Egyptian artefacts, and shipped them to Europe. This created a distinct impact on decorative artists and cabinetmakers, and was supported by the book of engravings *Voyage dans la Basse- et Haute-Egypte,* by French architect/engraver, Dominique Vivant Denon (published in 1802). This brought the exotic to the notice of domestic designers such as the Jacobs in France and Thomas Sheraton in England.

113. A Russian Mahogany Console Table and Pier Glass, c1810

The beauty of this piece lies in its purity of line and sparseness of decoration. The combination of mahogany and ormolu decoration is clearly influenced by French Empire – the clear grain markings of the 'flame' mahogany are featured around the mirror frame – and so too are the delicate winged-sphinx legs. The format of a pier glass above a console table was first perfected in the Palais de Versailles. The term 'pier' refers to the wall space between tall windows, and tables were designed to fill the gap.

Such clear French influence on Russian work is quite typical. Generally, furniture is only classified as Russian if documents still exist to prove Russian manufacture, as many pieces were made in France specifically for the Russian market during the 18th and early 19th centuries. After Napoleon's defeat by the armies of Tsar Alexander I (1801–25) in 1812, the threat of foreign invasion was lifted from Russia's shoulders. The Tsar sought to rebuild Russia's native furniture industry, and imported many foreign architects and designers to help. This led to a style which combined Empire and Biedermeier, of which The Palace of Pavlovsk near Leningrad is one of the best examples. By the mid 19th century, the quality of workmanship was declining all over Europe; Russia was no exception and it saw a brief Arts & Crafts revival as a reaction to lowering standards.

1800-1900

114. An English Regency Console Table, c1810

This is one of a pair of tables in the English Empire style, so called as it reflects the grandeur of that time. It is often sculptural, heavy and dark, although some pieces which are influenced by wider European taste have considerable gilt scrolling.

   The table is in the manner of Thomas Hope (1769–1831), an unusual and original man who was the son of a banker in Amsterdam. His family emigrated to Scotland at the end of the 18th century, and he later moved to London, where he displayed his collection of antiquities gathered on a Grand Tour of Europe and the Middle East between 1787 and 1795.

   Hope was a scholar and an architect, and his Greek, Roman and Egyptian artefacts were placed in a house which was furnished to his own designs with pieces such as this. His furnishings were often decorated with winged lions and masks to match the antiquities themselves.

   In 1807 Hope published his ideas and designs in *Household Furniture and Decoration* which, along with George Smith's *A Collection of Designs for Household Furniture and Interior Decorating,* influenced high Regency design well into the 19th century. It contrasted sharply with Robert Adam's neo-classical work, which had been so popular since the 1770s. On his death in 1831, Hope was buried in a mausoleum he himself designed at his country home of Deepdene in Surrey.

115. An Unusual English Regency Mahogany Library Table, c1810

The feature which distinguishes a library table from the often-similar centre table is its functional design. Drum library tables, for example, consist of a swivelling top which allows the reader to rotate it in search of a particular book, and generally library tables had drawers along both sides and at both ends.

   The unusual feature of this library table is that it has no drawers whatsoever, although the sides are panelled as if to simulate them. However, the top of this table consists of two hinged lids which, when opened, reveal undivided compartments clearly designed to hold folios of papers, such as maps, accounts or prints. (Bound into enormous books, architectural prints were very popular at this time, with artists such as Giovanni Battista Piranesi producing drawings of Italian villas or architectural details.) The reeded, splayed quadruped base of this piece is typical Regency, as is the cross-banded rosewood decoration.

116

117

114

115

116. An English Regency Marble-topped Table on a Gilt Wood Base, c1810

The Regency era's preoccupation with exotic colours and materials is nowhere more clearly illustrated than in 'specimen' marble-topped tables such as this. Invariably Italian-made, such circular pieces contained up to 200 different varieties of marble, in this case including *portoro, broccatello, verde antico, breccia, siena, rance* and many others.

The vogue for using different marbles began with 17th-century *pietra dura* work, a form of marble inlay fashioned in Baroque styles. These marble tops were expensive at the time, despite being produced in fairly large numbers, and were almost exclusively from Rome or Florence – the Carrara quarries north of Florence produce marble to this day.

The base of this piece is typical of these tables – the tops were so heavy that the support needed to be extremely sturdy. Here, this original period base consists of a stylized lotus pedestal ending in a trefoil platform on bun feet. It is unusual to find the original top with its base, as seen here, and in fact many of these tops were bought separately from the base at the time.

117. An Early 19th-century Mahogany Centre Table, c1810

The origin of this handsome table is unknown, although it is almost certainly European and probably French, English or Italian. Placed in a formal setting, a centre table such as this is more likely to have been used for display than as a functional dining or side table.

It is typical of the French Empire style (roughly equivalent to English Regency style, 1800–20), which was consistently revived in mainland Europe. Although this piece is dated c1810, it could have been made as a revival piece as late as 1860 or 1880. The brass edge to its top and brass stringing along the edge link it to the Regency period.

Two clues to its neo-classical influences are seen in the ormolu laurel-leaf decoration on the legs, and its cross-shaped trestles; the latter were used by both the Greeks and Romans in their furniture, as can be seen in surviving wall-paintings and decorated vases.

118. An American Federal Serving Table, *c*1810

A fine mahogany serpentine-fronted serving table, this piece was produced during a period in American Federal furniture history which corresponds to the English Regency. It was probably made in Salem, Massachusetts, by Samuel McIntire (1757–1811). He and John Seymour, a British cabinetmaker who emigrated in 1785, were dominant forces in Massachusetts furniture production at the end of the 18th century. They used excellent veneers, as seen here, and turned out beautifully finished pieces. As links with England weakened into the 19th century, their personal styles were more apparent in their furniture.

This table is elegant, with naturalistic carving on the flanking columns which sit above fluted legs. Carving such as this appears on other McIntire pieces, some of which may be seen in the Museum of Fine Arts in Boston. This American adaptation of architectural motifs retains much of a Regency, or Federal, feel, however, which is not surprising for a table from the English-orientated New England area. Salem contained a number of distinguished cabinetmakers at the beginning of the 19th century, including William Hook, Nehemiah Adams and the Sandersons.

119. An English Regency Rosewood Sofa Table, *c*1810

With the arrival of sofas in the drawing room during the Regency era, its 18th-century ancestor – the mahogany settee – was relegated to the hall, for some time its traditional location, where it was used by waiting guests. Along with the sofa came the accompanying sofa table, in this case made of the popular rosewood. Already strongly grained, the top is also cross-banded with satinwood and coromandel, and when highly polished would present a dazzling contrast. The frieze drawers, which are real on one side and blank on the other, are edged with stringing and have scrolling motifs which are echoed on both the ends and splayed legs of the table.

The clarity and simplicity of the line decoration prevent the table from seeming excessive. This type of ornament was recommended in Thomas Hope's *Household Furniture*, published in 1807, and other pattern-books of the time.

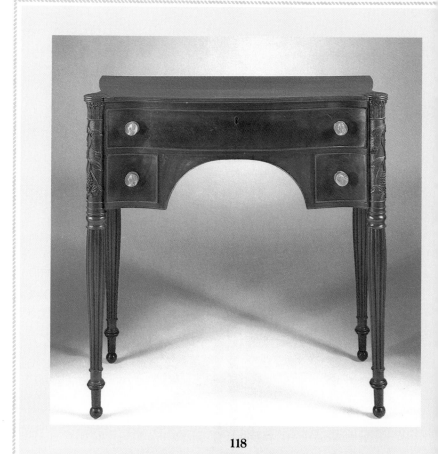

118

119

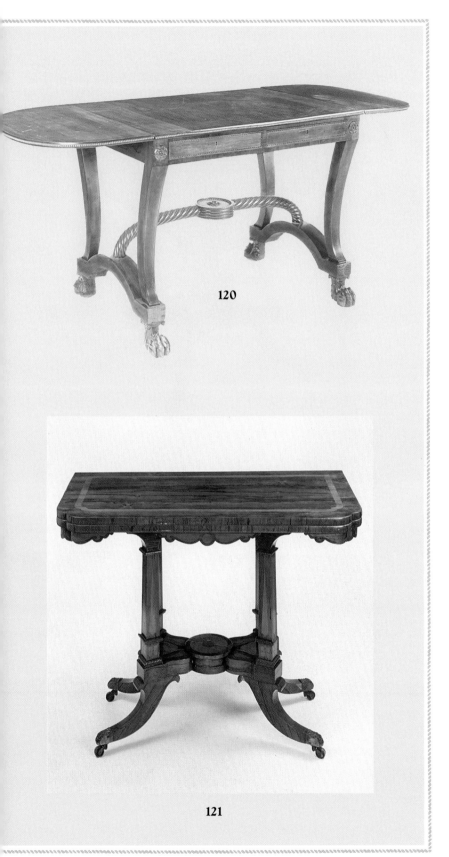

120

1800-1900

120. An English Regency Rosewood Sofa Table, c1815

This table is interesting for the unusual construction of its legs. At each end, two outward-curving sabre legs are joined by an arched stretcher and rest on substantial lion-paw feet. The two end stretchers are joined by a central rope-twist stretcher.

The rope-twist form of carving first appeared after Nelson's Battle of Trafalgar in 1805, during the Napoleonic wars with France ending at Waterloo in 1815. The motif became very popular, and was sometimes used on all the rails of a piece of furniture.

121. An English Regency Rosewood Card Table, c1815

Card tables use a number of different mechanisms to support their folding leaves – a concertina action, gate legs, swivel tops, envelope leaves, etc – but this table uses a unusual clock-like hinge. The two back legs swing out around a circular hinge (like the hands of a clock), which is hidden in a central capstan between the four legs, forming a cross shape. In fact, a join can be seen between the stable top half of the capstan, and the lower section, which hinges. The card table then folds out as normal.

Overall the piece is heavy, which dates it to late Regency. The top has a scrolled apron and is joined to the platform by four stout legs, supported in turn by four splayed legs. The legs are designed as columns, with capitals and pediments, and elsewhere there are traces of architectural details, with some naturalistic inlay.

121

122. An American Federal Work Table, Boston, Massachusetts, c1815

This elegant work table is attributed to the influential Massachusetts cabinetmakers, John and Thomas Seymour. Their work shows a preference for contrasting woods (in this case, mahogany, bird's-eye maple and flame birch); the piece is typically of high quality and neat proportions, and includes characteristic fluted legs and an emphasis on straight lines. The table is a combination of Georgian and Regency design, using elegant Hepplewhite inlay and broad neo-classical panels of colour. It is petite and very elegant, with fine deep carving of the mahogany.

The partnership was noted for inventive adaptations of European designs; the Winterthur Museum in Delaware has a famous desk which is labelled 'John Seymour and Son, Creek Lane, Boston' and dates from c1800. This is also based on a Hepplewhite design, and has a hybrid American use of inlay. It too has unusual neo-classical characteristics which might be considered slightly misplaced by English standards.

123. An English Regency Mahogany Drop-flap Work Table, c1815

This small sewing table shows all the Regency attributes which might be expected of this date. Decorated with dot-and-line brass inlay and its top cross-banded in rosewood, this practical table was fully equipped for its purpose: its main draw was sectioned into a sewing box, with compartments for cottons, needles, scissors and such like, and the 'sliding well' drawer made of fabric that hangs beneath would have held balls of wool, crocheting needles and other bulkier items.

Measuring only 18in (46cm) square, this dimunutive table, with its carved and scrolled support and elaborate sabre inlaid legs, has less appeal nowadays as sewing skills decline.

123

124

125

122

124. A Pair of English Regency Gilt Wood Console Tables, c1815

Purely decorative, console tables were designed to sit against a wall, often between windows, and as such became part of the room fittings rather than standing as individual pieces of furniture. Often large brackets with no other support, many had large mirrors above, filling wall space, and lent themselves to excessive ornamentation.

The use of the griffin (a winged lion with a bird's head) as a table support is typical of designers Thomas Hope and George Smith, and has become synonymous with Georgian excess. They are ideally adapted here as supports for their marble tops, which were a feature of the original console (or 'clap') tables of the early 18th century. Based on Italian prototypes, those early examples were often carved by Italian journeymen (travelling craftsmen) and were highly fashionable. Louis XVI's Palais de Versailles, the height of late 17th-century furniture styles, contains many examples of the marble-topped console table. They are an integral part of the decorative scheme, dividing the wall vertically into windows and mirrors in the *Galerie des Glaces*, (Gallery of Mirrors).

125. An Italian Empire Console Table, c1815

Many of the characteristic features of the Empire style seen here – the laurel leaves on the frieze, the heavy lion-paw feet, and the ornate horn-like fruiting legs – were in fact found in Italy before the end of the 18th century. However, it was not until the French Empire style of Napoleon's reign became popular that Italian workmen employed these features in a coherent way. The resulting style is known as Italian Empire.

The Bonaparte family were installed in force in Italy during Napoleon's reign. His brother, Joseph, became King of Naples, another brother, Lucien, was appointed Prince of Canino, and his sisters, Elisa, Caroline and Pauline, all married into leading families, the first two in Tuscany and Naples, respectively, and Pauline into the Roman Borghese family. Not only did this ensure the Bonapartes' power base, but it also spread the Napoleonic 'Empire' style to some impressive interiors. Elisa, for example, was responsible for importing French workmen to decorate several magnificent rooms in the Pitti Palace in Florence.

126. A French Empire Dining Table, *c*1815

A dining table such as this, designed to fold away when not in use, underlines the change in circumstance of the well-off in France after the Revolution. The Parisian bourgeois lived in much smaller homes than 50 years previously, partly due to a lack of space in Paris (where the French court had moved to from Versailles), partly to redistribution of aristocratic wealth, and so required furniture on an appropriate scale.

The ten legs of this table allow it to open out with a concertina action. The extending leaves – normally three but sometimes five – are supported by the central legs, both of which extend on a diamond-shaped frame. Typically Empire, the table is very plain, the top geometric, and the decoration on the frieze is restricted to finely figured wood. The legs are turned at the knee to create a 'knop' (collar) above the brass castors below.

Mahogany was the favoured wood of the Empire period (1804–15), despite the fact that a severe shortage made it extremely expensive. It was generally imported from mainland America and the West Indies, but the Continental Blockade imposed against the French in 1806 (when the English refused to export it from the territories they occupied) meant very little mahogany reached France.

127. An English Regency Sofa Table Attributed to George Bullock, *c*1815

This sofa table in the English Regency style is more substantial and impressive than its 18th-century predecessors. The influences of George Smith and Thomas Hope both can be seen here, the former in the chunky lion-paw feet and substantial pedestal, the latter in the brass inlay of exotic architectural patterns made so popular by Hope. This table top is squarer than earlier examples, which gives the piece weight, but it is lightened by the linear central column and ormolu mounts.

It is attributed to George Bullock (active between 1800 and 1820), who originally worked in Liverpool and Birmingham before setting up in London in 1815. Although much of Bullock's work was for the mass market, he also produced a large body of avant-garde designs, and is often thought of as an architect of the English Renaissance in the 19th century. His style became fully accepted in the 1930s and 1940s, but one of his major commissions was for the house of the metalworker, Matthew Boulton, at Great Tew in Oxfordshire. So many pieces were delivered to Boulton in 1817 that Bullock's bill ran to 42 pages.

128. A Pair of English Regency Mahogany Card Tables, *c*1815

Although it is difficult to date this pair precisely – they could have been manufactured any time between 1795 and 1815 – it seems likely from the turned legs that they were made after the turn of the century (square-sectioned legs and flat sides would indicate an earlier date).

During Regency times card tables started to appear in pairs, in fours and occasionally in larger sets. Generally made of mahogany, sometimes of satinwood, and others again in a combination of the two, card tables were occasionally made in woods such as oak, by provincial manufacturers.

These tables are of excellent quality, as well as being utilitarian and discreet – all the desirable qualities of so-called 'brown' furniture, which was made of mahogany and dated from the Georgian period, ending with the reign of George IV.

129. A French Empire Mahogany *Guéridon*, *c*1815

The *guéridon* in its original 17th-century form was a candlestick holder with a carved support; *guéridon* was the name given to young black pages at the courts of the time, and a common form of candleholder was the carved and painted form of a black page, many of whom were brought from the Moorish African coast for this purpose. During the 18th century the term expanded to include candlestands or small round tables (at this time the carving had disappeared), and by the end of the 1700s the table usually had two tiers. By this date, however, *guéridon* was used to refer to any round table.

This table is 4ft 3in (1.3m) across, and has a leather top for writing on. The drawers in its vertical, handsome frieze suggest that it might have been a library table. It is strikingly plain, but quite smart, and shows very little decoration apart from the gilt drawer knobs and the three 'hipped' cabriole legs ('hipped' refers to the sharp turning just above the knee).

The use of beautifully figured mahogany and the imposing effect of this table are reflections of the increased confidence and wealth of Napoleonic France. Interestingly, although France and England were at war at this time, the two leaders of furniture making were developing along very similar lines – this could almost be a Regency library table.

126

129

128

127

130. A Swedish Empire Console Table, c1815

The second half of the 18th century saw a long period of peace and prosperity in Scandinavia which was to be shattered by the Napoleonic wars. Sweden found itself caught between loyalties to France and England. The Bernadotte Dynasty, which still rules in Sweden today, descends from a marshal of Napoleon's who was invited to take the throne in the early 19th century; the destruction of the Danish fleet and half of Copenhagen by the English in 1801, however, was more than enough to persuade the Swedes to declare allegiance to England.

One effect of this was the development of a native furniture industry which took elements of design from both England and France; encouraged by interruption of sea traffic during the wars, Sweden had to rely more on its own production, and also saw considerable imports overland of furniture from Germany. The industry was helped by large quantities of high-quality native pine, which also gilt well; the small Scandinavian furniture-making industry which developed initially produced foreign designs, such as this one.

131. An English Late Regency or George IV Library Table, c1820

This library table has the distinguishing marks of a revolving top, and drawers on both sides. Many features of late Regency design are here, including the single turned column support, a platform leading to four sabre legs, and a fairly small base compared to the table top.

The use of rosewood and brass inlay can be seen on the strung drawers, and elsewhere on the form. The anthemion (or honeysuckle) decorative motif was popularized by Robert Adam, who originally took it from Roman architectural friezes, and revived by Thomas Hope in the early 18th century.

134

132

133

141. An English George IV Rosewood Games Table, *c*1830

In comparison with earlier games tables, this piece appears much heavier. This is partly due to the use of unrelieved rosewood – a dark wood when on its own – and also because of the departure from earlier neatness of line. The bulging compartment at one end of the table would have contained pieces for both backgammon and chess. The legs are no longer 'standard' Regency (splayed from one main column at each end) but stand separate, filled with delicately turned spindles, similar to designs produced by Gillow.

Two unusual features for a piece of this date are the gadrooned bottom of the games board section and the chunky paw feet with scrolling behind them. More at home on a piece of George II furniture, they are clues to the beginning of a revival of early Georgian styles.

142. An Ash Biedermeier Folding Breakfast Table, *c*1835

Probably Austrian or German, this table is typical of the Biedermeier style which was so popular in Europe (and particularly Austria, Germany and Eastern Europe) during the first half of the 19th century. The Biedermeier movement took its name from a fictional character who represented the typical German Philistine – which indicates the style's reaction against the 'aristocratic' past.

The lines in Biedermeier pieces are always clear and simple, and concentrate on the vertical and horizontal. This often gives a feeling of neo-classical simplicity, but sometimes leads to heaviness. With this table, the deep frieze and weight of the table top are balanced by the massive cubic feet on which the plain column legs are sitting.

Although Biedermeier can be thought of as an artistic movement (its most famous exponent being the self-taught artist, Carl Spitzweg, 1808–85), it mirrored a tendency throughout Europe to return to an uncluttered but dignified form. The combination of elements from English Regency, French Louis XVI and neo-classical styles led to a form that seemed to herald the Art Deco concentration on line.

141

142

1800-1900

143. An English William IV, or Victorian, Games and Work Table, c1840

This curious variant on the Georgian sewing table is made of walnut, a popular Victorian wood which came back into fashion in the mid 19th century. The top box held playing pieces for the board, and the well was for sewing equipment. On a Georgian piece, the well would have been a sliding drawer, but here it forms part of the central column, which rests on a squat, fluted baluster ending in three scrolling supports.

The piece is over-decorated compared to its Georgian equivalents – each black square on the board is decorated with geometric marquetry – and gives an overall bulbous impression.

144. An English William IV Pollard Oak Library Table, c1840

This table is a reminder of how fashions change – until the 1970s, heavy Victoriana such as this would have been quickly dismissed. But despite its lack of a named designer or cabinetmaker, which inevitably makes it less popular than other attributed pieces, furniture in this vein is becoming more desirable as earlier work becomes rarer.

Although this table was probably made during William IV's reign, it is difficult to date with accuracy. The beautiful pollard oak veneer reflects the Arts & Crafts Movement's revival of interest in native woods (oak being indigenous to Great Britain), and the flat table top with deep undecorated frieze has the flavour of German Biedermeier furniture of the 1820s, which encouraged bold, undecorated shapes. It is the trestle ends, carved, fluted, splayed feet, and baluster-turned stretchers which are an exaggeration of George IV or heavy Regency styles and give the piece its heavy look.

143

144

145

146

145. An English Victorian Papier Mâché Table, *c*1845

Papier mâché had been used in Persia (Iran) and the East for centuries before it was introduced to Europe in the 17th century. Made by moulding pressed paper or wood pulp mixed with glue and chalk, it was lightly polished once dry. The resulting dense and shiny surface took oil paint very easily. It is a similar finish to japanning, and sometimes hard to distinguish from lacquer; the main disadvantage to papier mâché is the difficulty in repairing furniture when chipped or otherwise damaged.

In 1772, Henry Clay of Birmingham, England, patented a form of the process, popularizing the little-known product in England. He produced numerous high-quality pieces, including a writing desk of 1784 found in Horace Walpole's London house in Strawberry Hill. The Birmingham company of Jennens and Bettridge, established in the late 18th century, became the most prolific producers of 19th-century papier mâché work, and this table is typical of their output. Furniture pieces included suites, settees, beds, pier tables and occasional tables such as this, and always carried their stamp. The firm employed many well-known artists of the day to paint scenes such as this on their work, among them John Frederick Herring (1795–1865), the celebrated sporting painter.

146. An Italian Renaissance Revival Writing Desk and Chair, *c*1850

After the fall of Napoleon Bonaparte in 1815, the Empire style continued to be popular in Italy, although it became diluted by various revivalist movements. One of these was the Renaissance revival, popular just before the *Risorgimento* (or unification of Italy) in the mid 19th century. In a sense, the Renaissance revival reflected a mood in Italy which was looking back to its 'finest hour' in design; in the same way, the Renaissance itself had revived the supremacy of Roman times.

In fact, this table is based on a Roman design (seen in wall-paintings made of marble) but its shape and decoration are taken from a Renaissance table style popular in the mid 16th century. The grotesque, swelling pedestals and loose cross-framed design reflect the Mannerist influences of the late Renaissance, and the supports are decorated just below the top with broad melon fluting which was much used on Renaissance chests. The overall effect, however, is clearly 19th century. The chair is late Empire style, and both pieces are lightened with floral marquetry characteristic of 19th-century Italian work.

147. A Mid 19th-century Florentine Black Marble Table on Gilt Wood Stand, c1850

Justly famous for its marble work since the 16th century, Italy was still considered a leader of art and learning in the middle of the 19th century. The precise craftsmanship shown in the micro-mosaic decoration here was admired throughout Europe, and this type of work was widely exported. Using hundreds of pieces of chipped marble and glass per square inch, the inlaid ovals depict various well-known Roman ruins and surround a familiar classical picture of doves drinking from a fountain, known as 'Pliny's Doves'. The table is edged with a band of malachite, a green mineral (sometimes used to veneer table tops) which takes its colour from copper traces.

The large gilt stand supporting the marble top has a structural, slightly Baroque feel to it; in fact, it could almost be 17th-century Venetian, and demonstrates that while furniture styles have changed considerably over the centuries, national characteristics endure. Several such tables were exhibited at the Great Exhibition of 1851 held at London's Crystal Palace and are recorded in the official catalogue.

148. An English Victorian Sutherland Table, c1850

Gate-leg tables had been made from the 16th century onward, and this six-legged form was established by the 17th century. Generally, the legs supported a round oak top, although this sophisticated version shows late Regency or Georgian influence in its rectangular leaves. The table has a surprisingly light feel to it, particularly as rosewood tables can be dull. It has a slender undercarriage and legs, both with fine turning, and the two centre legs are curiously joined by a horseshoe stretcher. This table is a specifically Victorian style which probably takes its name from the family which popularized it.

147

148

149. A 19th-century Scandinavian Pine Chamber Table, *c*1850

After Scandinavia's severe decline in power during the 18th and early 19th centuries, it became isolated, both geographically and in terms of trade, fashion, wealth and style. This meant that furniture designs remained fairly conservative, dominated either by European Empire styles or by the Scandinavian folk tradition; examples echoing the latter are often difficult to date.

This chamber table is of a characteristically simple construction; it has a functional drawer in the frieze, the legs are turned and the stretchers are heavy, much in the manner of a 17th-century English joint stool. The painting of the wood-grain effect on the drawer is typically German or Scandinavian, but was transferred to the United States, where it still survives, by that country's Central European immigrants. Nineteenth-century pine was of much better quality than today's, as the trees were older and more mature; thus furniture of this period endured well.

149

1800-1900

The Crystal Palace Exhibition, London, 1851

In England in 1851, largely thanks to the efforts of Prince Albert, Queen Victoria's husband, an exhibition of products from all over the world was organized at Crystal Palace. Furniture designs and other decorative objects in a variety of styles from the mid 19th century were extensively exhibited. The massive display was housed in the especially built Crystal Palace, an elaborate and revolutionary structure erected in London's Hyde Park and made of glass panels on a steel frame. Its arched roof stood more than three storeys high, and it contained fountains, sculpture, trees and pavilions on different themes from different countries. The catalogue of the Exhibition produced by *The Art-Journal* – more than 300 pages long and containing over 1,000 illustrations – provides an intriguing commentary on Victorian taste. Ralph Wornum (1812–77) wrote an editorial essay in the catalogue discussing style, decoration and excess which is still relevant today. He was critical of excessive ornament and of the naturalist school (which used design motifs taken from nature), and dismissive of the revival movements (such as Rococo and Gothic), which presented some exceedingly heavy compositions.

'Ornament run riot' can certainly be seen in these catalogue entries. But arguments against natural motifs, central to 19th-century design, were sometimes contrived; arguing that nature should not change the structure of a piece perhaps simply shows a preference for neo-Classicism. At least, however, design has moved away from Empire styles worldwide. The Victorian style, which these prints illustrate, seems to be distinct from the past, albeit heavy, and perhaps it can be said to have paved the way for Art Nouveau.

150. Table by J & W Hilton of Montreal, *c*1851

'Amongst the contributions of our fellow subjects in Canada,' reads the catalogue, 'there are some specimens highly creditable to her manufacturers.' These included an elegant fire engine, a sleigh and this table. It comes from French-speaking Canada and accurately reflects Central European tastes of the time. There are few straight lines, the legs are scrolled, the top is irregular and carved with foliage, etc, and the stretchers meet in a pseudo-classical urn. It is made of 'boldly carved' black walnut.

151. An English Console Table and Frame for Mirror with Bracket, *c*1851

These were made by the Gutta Percha Company, which was set up in London to manufacture objects made of the new composition, gutta percha. This 'natural plastic' was derived from the juice of Malayan trees, which provided an amorphous white substance that could be moulded into various shapes. In this case, it has been moulded onto a wire armature to form an extravagantly Victorian example of a Rococo console table and mirror above. It is exactly the style of furniture that Ralph Wornum so objected to in his commentary on the exhibits at the Great Exhibition, its decoration being both excessive and rather improbable.

152. An Ebony Table by Doe Hazelton & Co of Boston, Massachusetts, *c*1851

This table draws upon a number of different sources. The front legs are reminiscent of furniture by William Kent, the early 18th-century English designer, who commonly used herm figures (half-human, half-architectural) such as these. The scrolling stretchers which support a vase of flowers have a Rococo feel, as does the apron's central cartouche, with its mask head. Circling the apron is a naturalistic ornament of a flowering vine, and the top is typically Victorian with its irregular shape. It is carved in ebony, the darkness of which would increase the heavy effect. Eighteenth-century American furniture drew heavily on European styles, a trend which continued into the 19th century, as an international style evolved.

153. The Crusader Chess Table from Ireland, *c*1851

This table is the work of a Mr Graydon of Dublin, and is historical revivalism at its most extreme. Its extraordinary shape has four lobes surrounding the central square and bowing sides. It is decorated with relief work such as that found on the Parthenon, but here showing the medieval Crusaders in their battle against Islam. The legs – or corner pillars – each stand on four columns directly taken from Romanesque architecture, which was popular in Europe during the 11th century. Plucking decorative motifs from many different centuries and countries, this table is enthusiastic, if not tasteful.

151

150

152

153

154. An 'Elizabethan' Table and Stool, *c*1851

This ensemble was made by the Englishman, C J Richardson, who according to the Great Exhibition catalogue was 'known by his excellent work on Elizabethan ornament and furniture, in which he has with much perseverance and ability pointed out the peculiarities and rich fantasies visible in this school of design. He has now practically realised his knowledge . . . ' Fully fledged Renaissance Revival, this table is probably most closely based on a combination of 1550s Italian design and English styles of fifty to a hundred years later; the mask head and decoration on the trestle ends are similar to a chair in the Victoria & Albert Museum, London, designed by a Frenchman in the 1640s. Typically Victorian, this bears little resemblance to any work from the reign of Elizabeth I (which ended in 1603) or immediately after, but draws on an impressive medley of sources and styles.

155. An Italian Table Made for the King of Sardinia, *c*1851

This table was made by G Capello of Turin and is basically Empire-style. It is based on classical ideals – a square shape, simple dignified decoration on its top and neo-Classical pedestal with anthemion motif. Italy generally is thought of as excessive in its decoration, but these pieces are fairly restrained in terms of ornament.

156. A 19th-century Table by Michael Thonet of Vienna, *c*1851 and

157. A Neo-Rococo Austrian Table by Carl Leistler, *c*1851

The table by Michael Thonet (1796–1871) has an unusual construction: it is made of bent rosewood, which is shaped so that the grain of the wood follows the line of curve required; rather than relying on mortice-and-tenon joints or screws and nails, it concentrates on the elasticity of the wood (which was bent under intense steam to allow it to be manipulated in this way). Thonet was famous for his bentwood chairs, made in the millions and still manufactured today.

The bentwood table is in complete contrast to the more conventional table by Leistler, manufacturer of furniture in the 'later Venetian taste', which uses some of the Baroque decoration of the late 17th and 18th centuries – elaborate scrolling, loose natural forms and heavy construction. Interestingly, Thonet and Leistler were at one time business partners: in the 1840s they supplied furniture

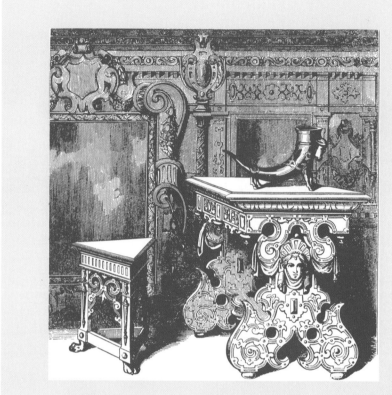

154

156

158

155

157

to Prince Liechtenstein.

These two tables are from exactly the same date, but whereas Leistler's looks backward for inspiration, Thonet's looks toward the 20th century.

158. An English Cast-iron Deerhound Table, c1855

This cast-iron table was made by the Coalbrookdale Company, which was established in the 18th century by Abraham Darby. It produced many notable works during the Industrial Revolution, including the Severn Gorge Bridge of 1779, and continued well into the 19th century, producing both industrial pieces and even domestic bronze sculpture. In the second half of the 19th century, the company reproduced a large variety of French bronze animal sculpture, made by Coalbrookdale in cast iron which was patinated to simulate the original. Such experience provided the necessary skills to make this astonishing ensemble.

This table, exhibited at the *Exposition Universelle* in Paris in 1855, was designed by John Bell, who was influenced by the English Victorian sculptors, John Flaxman and Francis Chantrey. A student at the Royal Academy, Bell exhibited there until 1879 and produced some fairly well-known sculptures, such as *The Eagle Slayer*. The arms on the dogs' collars here are of the Hargreaves family in Lancashire, for whom the table was made; it was probably the property of Colonel John Hargreaves of Whalley Abbey.

Coalbrookdale produced catalogues of their wares, and this table appeared in the 1860 edition, listed at a price of £80. It may well be unique, as no others are known; it is now in the Ironbridge Gorge Museum in Shropshire.

159. A 19th-century Dutch Marble-inlaid Table, c1860

This 19th-century revival of a Rococo table (originally produced in the first half of the 18th century) makes the most of the Dutch passion for ebony or ebonized furniture. (Ebonized furniture consisted of black lacquer-painted furniture, made to look like ebony.) Exotic materials such as tortoiseshell, ivory and marble were extracted from countries occupied by the Dutch during the 17th century, and were often combined with ebony to produce a lighter finish overall.

The sculptural effect and apron carving of this table were very much to Victorian taste, and a number of these were exported around Europe. The style of the cabriole legs and pierced stretcher dates from c1720, and the top shows a variety of marble *pietra dura* work, almost always imported from Italy. By the mid 19th century, however, many of the fine stones found in early *pietra dura* mosaic had been exhausted, and the marble inlay here is distinctly dull in comparison with earlier work. Around this time, many marble pictures were mass-produced, and were generally of a lower quality.

160. A 19th-century Austrian Porcelain *Guéridon, c1860*

The fashion for porcelain furniture was inspired by the 19th-century passion for decoration. This piece is made with porcelain from the Vienna factory, and is decorated with gilt scrolls and precisely modelled fruiting vines on its stem.

Porcelain furniture had a great advantage over wood in both carving and gilt work. Its harder surface could be modelled with far more detail, and gilt – and other bright fired-on glazes – could be applied directly to its surface. (Gesso has to be applied to wood before the gilt, or else the polychrome is absorbed.) Porcelain was obviously more fragile, though, and pieces such as this were often held together with internal metal rods and brackets.

Austria at this time was at the centre of the Austro-Hungarian Empire, which covered much of the Northern Mediterranean. The hand-painted decoration on the table top shows rustic scenes from the more exotic corners of the Empire, including Hungary and Dalmatia. Labelled with the name of each area they represent, they are extremely precise in their detail.

160

162

161

159

161. An English Victorian Burr Walnut Centre Table, *c*1860

Despite the first impression this table gives of being heavy and dull, it has a top made of intricate burr walnut. Like pollard oak, burr walnut was a specially chosen cross-section used for veneer because of its attractive pattern. If it was highly polished, the effect of this table would be very different, drawing attention away from the bulbous legs and toward the fine grain of the wood and the carved ivy border along the table's shaped edge.

The unusual angle of this photograph emphasizes what Eero Saarinen (the Finnish-American 20th-century architect) called 'a slum of legs'. The table's four scrolled legs and supports surround a central turned finial sitting on an octopus-like platform. The whole of the bottom half of the table is covered with scrolling, possibly a precursor of organic Art Nouveau decoration.

Although it is difficult to imagine why such heavy styles were ever ordered or made, this table was based on past design (the carving could be seen as the death throes of George IV or Chippendale decoration); and popular taste, then as now, often preferred safer, established designs to more recent developments.

162. A French Tulipwood and Porcelain Mounted Writing Table, *c*1860

This writing table in the style of Louis XVI, popular a hundred years earlier, shows the characteristic combination from that time of tulipwood and porcelain plaques. Originally these plaques came from the newly established Sèvres porcelain factory (*c*1750). They were decorative, rectangular set pieces of a floral or rustic peasant-in-a-landscape pattern on white, surrounded with a gilt border and on an overall background colour, such as the green used here.

Simon-Philippe Poirier and Dominique Daguerre, two Parisian furniture dealers, specialized in producing pieces exactly like this in the mid 18th century, employing many known craftsmen such as Martin Carlin (d.1785), who excelled in this style. Many of the pieces were dated, and this table is typical of those produced *c*1765.

The table's only concession to its real date of *c*1860 is the fact that its size and proportions have been reduced to accommodate 19th-century living styles.

1800-1900

95

163. A 19th-century Italian Marquetry Breakfast Table, *c*1865

This spectacular table is inlaid with various woods on an ebony background. The central floral pattern is surrounded by strapwork, embellished with scrolls and trailing flowers. Italy had a long history of high-quality marquetry which dated back to the 16th century. This form shows certain similarities with *pietra dura* (stone inlay) work for which both Florence and Rome were renowned, and the decoration is based on many of the same motifs.

The edge of the table is finished with a gadrooned brass band, and the whole top sits on a single column with a trefoil base. It tips on its side for storage, as all breakfast tables do, and probably also to display its distinctive design.

164. An English Victorian Inlaid Dining Table, *c*1867

Although this table is sturdy compared to Georgian pieces, it shows the beginnings of a movement to abandon the excessive scrolling and clumsiness of earlier Victorian tables. The top is made of amboyna, a light wood, and is bordered with fine-quality marquetry. The legs and support are neatened with straight edges, and the central column uses parallel lines to suggest fluting. The ebony stringing of the edges, both on the top and the undercarriage, gives the table a smarter, lighter feel.

The undercarriage, with its square-sectioned members, is slightly reminiscent of late 17th-century design, although the oval top is a typical 19th-century shape. The marquetry on the top shows the monogram 'AM', of the original owner, displayed in four cartouches around the table edge. It was made for Alfred Morrison and displayed at the Paris Exposition of 1867.

165. A 19th-century Louis XV-style Writing Table, *c*1870

The mid 19th century saw a vogue throughout Europe for revivals of all dates. One of the favourites was Louis XV, and despite being made up of curious parts, this table is very much in the spirit of mid 18th-century designs. It has a tulipwood background, it is decorated with marquetry and the top is edged in brass. However, the stretcher and stand supporting the legs at each end are clumsier than those elements on the elegant writing tables of the 18th century.

The table is stamped with the name of its 19th-century maker, Gardiennet, and is well made. Many revival pieces were direct copies, taken from actual pieces or pattern-books, but some makers found it impossible to resist making 'improvements'.

163

164

167

165

166

166. An English Victorian Mahogany Writing Table, *c*1880

This quality reproduction of a Louis XVI writing desk bears the stamp of Edwards & Roberts of Broadmoor St., London. Working toward the end of the 19th century, the company specialized in manufacturing several revival styles, such as the piece here and Edwardian breakfront bookcases. The original Louis XVI style, which flourished roughly a hundred years earlier, was a plainer reaction to elaborate Rococo designs, and was influenced by English taste of the time. In many cases, Edwards & Roberts would follow the original drawings and produce virtually identical reproductions of a piece, but in this case there are obvious adaptations to suit Victorian tastes.

The use of ormolu to emphasize the fluting on the legs and the edge of the table top are typical of the original style. But the lack of expensive, high-quality veneer in the Victorian era accounts for the use of lighter woods, giving a lighter feel to the piece. The dark wood used here is mahogany, the lighter, amboyna – a West Indian wood with a tight, swirling grain. As on authentic Louis XVI pieces, the table's sides are decorated with banding, but the scrolling marquetry on the top is Victorian. Although the piece is well made, it misses the feel of true Louis XVI furniture.

167. A 19th-century Writing Table, *c*1890

This is a clear copy of the Louis XVI style of a century before, popular in France in the 1770s and 1780s, the last two decades before the Revolution. Probably made in France or England, it also could have originated in Italy or Germany, which also had long traditions of fine marquetry and cabinetmaking.

The tulipwood cross-banding and trellis-and-dot veneer on the table top and sides are typical late 18th-century French decoration, but on close inspection adjustments have been made to the original style. It is slightly smaller than a similar piece from a century earlier, probably because late 19th-century homes were not as palatial as the châteaux for which an original would have been destined. The inlaid leather top tends to be a later feature, and the brass fittings seen here would have been fire-gilded ormolu work. This complex process involves applying melted gold to bronze; lethal fumes are given off, but the technique results in a truly gilt effect, one which is then hand-finished. In the 19th century, it was replaced by a cheaper electrical process, similar to silver-plating, which never really achieves the same result.

1900
TO
1999

Charles Rennie Mackintosh designed the library of the Glasgow School of Art in the early 20th century. He was the first to question seriously the basis of furniture and interior architecture, beginning a century of radical change from Art Nouveau to Bauhaus.
On the chair backs, as on the supporting piers, there are geometric patterns, and functional structures are not disguised but displayed. However, wood grain is concealed by dark staining.

Since 1900, explosive changes in fashion and art have produced a wide and confusing range of tables, varying from revived antique styles in the Chippendale vein to modernist towers of plate glass. A simple way of placing a table within a sensible context is by asking the question: 'Is this table made up mostly of clean, straight lines, or is it curved and decorated with rich patterns, exotic wood grain and carving?' These two types of tables swing in and out of favour over the first half of the century, and indeed afterward.

The Arts & Crafts firms of the 19th century such as Morris and Co had brought craftsmanship back into fashion, thereby influencing the 'straight clean line' table makers of the early 20th century. These included the Glaswegian Charles Rennie Mackintosh (1868–1928), whose famous black, high-backed chairs were complemented by tables with plain lacquered or painted finishes, a minimum of decoration and often of a size rather grand and unfriendly, as well as the American Frank Lloyd Wright (1867–1959) and Josef Hoffmann (1870–1956) in Vienna. Hoffmann and his colleague Koloman Moser founded the Wiener Werkstätte (Viennese Workshops), which produced – commercially if somewhat expensively – designer tables of black, white and metal grids during the first 20 years of the century. The students from that workshop carried the gospel of the straight line all over Europe.

In 1915 in the Netherlands the De Stijl movement applied the affection for rectilinearity, primary colours and flat surfaces to furniture making; Gerrit Rietveld (1888–1964) made geometric-shaped tables which even today seem revolutionary. In Germany Bauhaus students concentrated on new materials and techniques, creating Machine Age tables of tubular steel, with glass tops and often no decoration save a chrome finish to the metal. Likewise, in Finland Alvar Aalto (1899–1976) experimented with novel uses for plywood, perfecting this material with new woods and glues and producing moulded tables and trolleys from one or very few parts. Crucial advances were being made using this and other new materials and methods, and the increasing use of plastics led to a preponderance of synthetic tables.

The other branch of Art Nouveau was French in origin, its two design centres being Paris and Nancy where Emile Gallé (1846–1904) produced handsome vases with sensuous curves and in vivid colours; he began to manufacture tables, chairs and case pieces with similar lines and nature-inspired embellishments in the 1880s. The flat tops of his tables were of irregular shapes, often inlaid with landscapes, blossoms and twisting stems; their legs likewise were rarely straight but instead were carved, in some cases like spreading vines, in others as massive dragonflies. Parisian Hector Guimard (1867–1942) designed tables with undulating curves, very much akin to his ornate wrought-iron entrances to the Paris Metro. Victor Horta (1861–1947), the Belgian architect, designed curving, looping tables for his similarly decorated buildings, as did Antonio Gaudí (1852–1926) of Barcelona, whose amorphous, anthropomorphic shapes feature knobby knees and crooked elbows, sometimes with wrought-iron supports.

The distinction between tables with straight lines and those with curves and decoration adapted from nature extends into the Art Deco period, although the latter elements become much more stylized and less organic in the 1920s. Indeed, there was a reaction against the swirling plant forms of Gallé and his Nancy colleagues, and a new and very expensive style emerged from Paris, reaching its peak at the 1925 *Exposition des Arts Décoratifs* there. Premier *ébéniste* Emile-Jacques Ruhlmann (1879–1933) made tables with outswept legs terminating in neat brass feet (or *sabots*) which echoed French 18th-century styles and were often of the same high quality as their Louis XV and XVI predecessors, using precious patterned woods. Designers turned to rich materials, both traditional and exotic, including lacquer, snakeskin, marble and sharkskin. Jacques-Henri Lartigue, for instance, supported a table on a striking sphere of marble and Rose Adler inlaid a black-lacquer table with *coquille d'oeuf* (crushed eggshell, an Oriental innovation). Such Parisian furniture tended to use conventional materials and be based on styles from Louis XV to tribal African. But there was stiff competition, in the form of tubular-metal, Machine Age furniture, and antique reproduction styles, constantly popular.

Post-war furniture benefited from both new design technologies and materials (particularly plastic), as well as from the travelling of furniture designers and craftsmen for the reconstruction of war-ravaged buildings and furniture. Milan took on increasing importance, as designers such as Carlo Mollino (1905–1973) produced light-hearted economical tables. The usage of plywood increased, alone or combined with other materials, such as Formica (a laminated plastic). The Milan designers developed an optimistic style whose tables featured light constructions and bright colours. Throughout the 1960s and up to the present day, Italy has produced not only functional but also visually exciting tables, the designs of Ettore Sottsass (b.1917) for the Memphis group foremost among them.

With their built-in strength, plastic and fibreglass allowed new furniture shapes to be moulded. Charles Eames (1907–1978), one of the most influential American furniture designers of the century, experimented with plywood during World War II, and afterward produced a monochromatic, single-pedestal table, all made of glass reinforced polyester – a truly novel creation. Great Britain also produced good-quality tables, especially in the no-frills, traditional vein, such as those by Gordon Russell (1892–1980), whose sturdy forms looked back to 19th-century Arts & Crafts furniture. The Swinging Sixties, on the other hand, gave birth to bizarre Pop Art tables, such as Allen Jones's *Table Sculpture,* whose base is a crouching, sado-masochistic woman; this is a good example of how new materials (painted glass fibre and resin) allowed the return of tables based on shapes and curves.

In the 1980s there are two main streams: tables made for use, such as may be bought in any large store and are relatively inexpensive to make, utilizing new materials and methods. In this competitive market, home assembly is often a way of reducing the retail price even further. As ever, antique reproductions of earlier styles, particularly English Georgian and French Louis XV, abound and are much more affordable than the originals.

Secondly, tables are still made for art's sake: Danny Lane creates his from stacks of glass, not intending them to be functional, but 'sculptural'. Another example of designer tables, but much more utilitarian, are the revivals of early 20th-century designs: Hoffmann and Mackintosh reproductions are popular, as the discerning consumer wants to inject more style into his or her home or office. Then there are the small-scale designer-craftsmen who are not sufficiently well known or innovative to appear in the press or in books such as this one, but who make good tables simply because they want to follow in the self-assured footsteps of centuries of tradition.

168. A French Revivalist Tulipwood and Ormolu Library Table, *c*1900

The French passion for revivalist 18th-century furniture reached its peak during the reign of Napoleon III, *c*1860. At first, good quality, authentic pieces were made, but after a while fidelity to the original patterns and spirit waned.

This table, produced around the turn of the century, is similar in some ways to an English centre table. It has a deep frieze, sits · on a quadruped support similar to those of around 1830 and is excessively covered with Rococo ormolu decoration – too much even for a piece from the height of the Louis XV era. The overall effect is overdecorated and gauche.

169. An Edwardian Georgian Revival Mahogany Octagonal Centre Table, *c*1905

The beginning of the 20th century was ripe with new designs and designers worldwide, but the largest single area of furniture production was still revivalist. Interest in the revival of earlier styles existed widely in Europe. In France, the 19th-century concern with royal revivals of Louis XIV, XV and XVI styles continued until well into the 20th century; in Great Britain, the Edwardians turned to Georgian designs, based on the styles of Chippendale, Sheraton and Hepplewhite.

This table is a classic example of the revivalist trend and is fairly close to its true Georgian counterpart, differing in two main areas. The stretchers are more elaborate than on a typical Georgian piece, and the decoration is decidedly more excessive. The Edwardians' taste for floral inlay takes the place of the Georgians' more reserved crossbanding, and where boxwood marquetry would have been separated but perhaps in a panel on an original piece, here the boxwood marquetry is placed straight onto the mahogany base.

171

169

170

168

170. An Edwardian Oval Satinwood Painted Table, *c*1910

Although it is hard to fault this beautifully executed revival of a Georgian painted table on any one feature, a series of small clues suggest a later date. The construction of the undecorated wood frame would date it accurately, although it is impossible to see from a photograph. On a Georgian piece of this delicacy, the veneer would have been a better quailty than the wood used here – probably of a dazzling pale colour with beautiful figuring. The painted decoration in Hepplewhite style is slightly too bright and elaborate, and covers too large an area. Also, the small oval form with two tiers is an unusual Georgian combination.

All of these factors make it likely that the table dates to the late 19th or early 20th century, although copies are sometimes so good that it is impossible to be sure.

171. A French Art Nouveau 'Grotesque' Table by Emile Gallé, *c*1895

Emile Gallé (1846–1904) was a prominent founding member of the Nancy school of Art Nouveau design, based in Lorraine. Most of his output was in glass and ceramic: his cameo-glass vases with relief designs are perhaps his best-known work. Gallé produced furniture from the mid 1880s onward, inspired in part by his visit to a stockist of exotic woods. He felt that Art Nouveau motifs should be applied to conventional construction, thus believing that individuality lay in ornamentation. Hence he used blank surfaces for his subtle floral decoration.

This table is in the 'organic' style of Art Nouveau, which is highly ornamented with swirling lines and a variety of natural motifs, eg, entomological and botanical. On its upper and lower tiers, fine inlay of many different woods appears in a natural surrounding – such delicate marquetry with a lack of perspective was one of Gallé's hallmarks. The hybrid animal/insect figures on the table legs here are similar to the neo-classical sphinx, but depicted in a typical Art Nouveau manner.

1900-1999

172. A French Art Nouveau Table by Edward Colonna, c1895

The work of Edward Colonna (1862–1948), one of the designers connected to the Paris atelier set up by S Bing, whose *Maison de l'Art Nouveau* gave the turn-of-the-century style its name, is representative of the Parisian school of Art Nouveau. Whereas the Nancy designers produced rather heavy work, the Parisian group (which also included Eugène Gaillard and Georges de Feure) tended to employ simpler, lighter structures, often with a minimum of decoration. The German-born Colonna was also involved with Bing's Pavillon de l'Art Nouveau at the Paris 1900 Exposition, where he jointly decorated six rooms with Georges de Feure. He also worked in Belgium and the United States.

173. A French Art Nouveau Corner Table by Georges de Feure, c1900

This table contains several of Art Nouveau's classic features – supports in the form of stylized flowers, an odd shape with every surface decorated and a concentration on the sinuous line. Georges de Feure (1868–1928) collaborated with Edward Colonna and Eugène Gaillard; all three were associated with S Bing. De Feure's furniture is often of gilt wood, decorated with a floral motif. He also worked as a painter, lithographer, engraver and ceramicist, taught at the Paris Ecole des Beaux-Arts, and exhibited in a variety of media at important European exhibitions.

174. A French Art Nouveau Side Table with Tea Tray by Hector Guimard, c1900

This walnut table has a matching tea tray with bronze handles, and is typical of the chic Parisian school of Art Nouveau, as opposed to the heavier, provincial Ecole de Nancy. It is beautifully carved with smooth, elegant lines, giving the impression of a piece of sculpture rather than furniture, and is a fine example of Hector Guimard's innovation, which often extended across different media – here, glass, bronze and wood blend together to become an integral part of the design.

Guimard (1867–1942) was the leading French architect of Art Nouveau and introduced Victor Horta, the radical Belgian architect, to Paris. Guimard's most lasting monuments are the sinuous entrances to the Paris Metro, which to most visitors symbolize exotic *fin-de-siècle* Paris.

Guimard saw architecture and furniture as a whole, and hence designed many interiors and furnishings, as well as the exteriors, of several buildings.

175. A French Art Nouveau Room Designed by Georges Hoentschel, c1905

This room by the Parisian architect/potter/designer, Georges Hoentschel (1855–1915), illustrates the organic quality of French Art Nouveau – the top of the table here is a conventional rectangle quartered to match veneers, but the legs have a naturalistic design: taken almost directly from nature, they are in the form of branches.

The Art Nouveau style appealed very much to the architectural discipline, and designing a whole room with sympathetic characteristics was good architectural logic. In this room, for example, it is clear that the glass-fronted cabinet matches the table and chairs. Similarly, the combination of dining table, chairs and vitrines is a traditional one, emphasizing the point that Art Nouveau decoration was generally applied to traditional forms in good-quality woods.

176. A French Writing Table and Chair by Louis Majorelle, c1910

Majorelle (1859–1926) was a prominent member of the Nancy school of design, a group of French architects and designers who promoted 'organic' Art Nouveau. Emile Gallé, famous for his glassware and ceramics, was active in founding the school, which is closely associated with the area around Nancy in northeastern France.

Majorelle originally trained as a painter before taking over his father's furniture business in the late 1870s. His speciality was sophisticated furniture such as that for up-market Paris restaurants like Chez Maxim, and although his early furniture was traditional, he was quick to adopt the nature-inspired forms of Art Nouveau. Much of his work is in fairly dark hardwoods, such as mahogany or walnut, with decoration on the upholstery or on the sides and drawers of tables, as here. This is relatively restrained for Majorelle, but then its date is quite late.

172

173

176

174

175

177. Scottish Furniture by Charles Rennie Mackintosh, *c*1900

Both the interior of this room and its furniture were designed by the Glaswegian architect/ designer, Charles Rennie Mackintosh (1868–1928). Among his sources were those employing strong vertical lines with horizontal grids, as well as the massive forms associated with the Scottish baronial tradition. The Japanese influence is shown through his simple, undecorated designs; he tended to ebonize his pieces, such as the table illustrated, in order to eradicate any sign of natural wood grain, and decoration was restrained, often simply cut out, as seen on the cupboards on the wall in this room.

Mackintosh's concern with minimal decoration and curve was in fact one of the main forces behind the conversion to line rather than form, an idea expanded by Josef Hoffmann and others in Vienna and Frank Lloyd Wright in the United States. Mackintosh was primarily an architect, and among his limited output of 14 buildings was the Glasgow School of Art, which shows his progression from the organic forms associated with the Art Nouveau style to the linear, geometric forms of proto-modernism (the building was completed in stages).

This ebonized table is based on medieval principles – it is extremely heavily built, plain timbered and virtually undecorated. It is arched between the legs, and is very dignified and monumental.

178. A Scottish White Painted Table by Charles Rennie Mackintosh, *c*1900

This table is quite unlike Mackintosh's atmospheric, medievalizing work. Among his 'friendlier' domestic pieces were several white chairs and tables with an enamel-like surface. This was obtained by a coach-painting technique, which was very smooth and similar to lacquer.

This example has an enamel glass inset to contrast with the large flat surface. The table legs broaden toward the floor, a form emphasizing the vertical lines and complementing the elliptical shape of the top. It structure clearly shows Mackintosh's architectural influences.

177

178

59

180

179

181

179, 180 & 181. Austrian Tables by Josef Hoffmann, 1901–1910

Like Frank Lloyd Wright in America (1867–1959), the Viennese Josef Hoffmann (1870–1956) actively worked through several periods – Art Nouveau, Art Deco and the Modern movement. Hoffmann was a member of the Vienna Secession, founded in 1897, and cofounded the Wiener Werkstätte (or Vienna workshops) in 1903. Design of the turn-of-the-century period generally splits into two categories, the organic Art Nouveau school, whose motifs were based on forms such as the curves of a plant, and the geometric, linear branch, of which Hoffmann was an exponent, which concentrates on straight lines, contrasting colours and the formation of grids to define space. Hoffmann was much inspired by Scotsman Charles Rennie Mackintosh (1868–1928), who supported the Secession movement and its members.

The Wiener Werkstätte were set up to manufacture the new design styles in Vienna, and the enterprise proved enormously successful over several decades, producing mainly expensive furniture for an elite clientèle.

Around 1900, the beginnings of Hoffmann's move away from conventional curvilinear furniture were seen in the interiors of houses he designed, such as the Palais Stoclet in Brussels. This new style of furniture was also shown at the Paris exhibitions, influential platforms for innovative ideas. Table number 179, designed in 1901, shows Hoffmann adapting traditional forms with straight lines and new materials, smooth surfaces of stained wood, and with metal details for effect and strength.

As he became better known as a designer, Hoffmann's commissions varied greatly; table number 180 was designed for Kabarett Fledermaus, a theatre-bar in Vienna. It is strongly geometric, and uses typically smooth surfaces and restrained colour (later pieces from the 1920s and 1930s are more rounded). The model (number 181) retains the straight line, and is a classic geometric design which is still made today by the German firm, Franz Wittmann, which reproduces several other chairs and tables by Hoffmann.

182. The Elephant Trunk Table by Adolf Loos, *c*1902

This table was exhibited at the Vienna Secession in 1902; it was designed by the Austrian architect/designer, Adolf Loos (1870–1933). Also known as the Spider table, it is made of walnut with copper fittings around the lobed top and copper feet on the legs. Although not functional, the table has an intriguing design whose legs are supported on half circles appearing to combine Oriental inspiration, an interest in geometric shapes, and cabriole legs. The Vienna Secession was known for its acceptance of the new, the original and the good; this feeling for exploration and enquiry led to the Secession's, and later the Wiener Werkstätte's, leading position in the history of turn-of-the-century design.

Adolf Loos studied with Otto Wagner, an architect and *éminence grise* of the Secession, and also created designs for the influential Thonet factory, which specialized in bentwood furniture.

183. An Art Deco Partners' Desk and Chair, *c*1915

This functional writing desk and chair show how stylish Art Deco ideas could be incorporated into practical design. Although luxurious and high-quality work, the table's use of fruitwood veneer is not unusual, its tapering legs are not excessive and the repeated coil decoration is minimal.

It is probably the work of Paul Iribe (1883–1935), who was noted for his use of similar coils, and who was considered one of the more moderate of the avant-garde Art Deco artists. His interesting career included illustrating for design magazines; founding the magazine, *Le Témoin (The Witness)*, in 1905; designing jewellery, fabrics, interiors and advertisements; and working for Jaques Doucet in his Paris apartment on the Avenue de Bois. Having travelled to the United States in 1914 to work with the film producer-director Cecil B De Mille, he returned to France in the 1930s and was for some time associated with Coco Chanel.

184

182

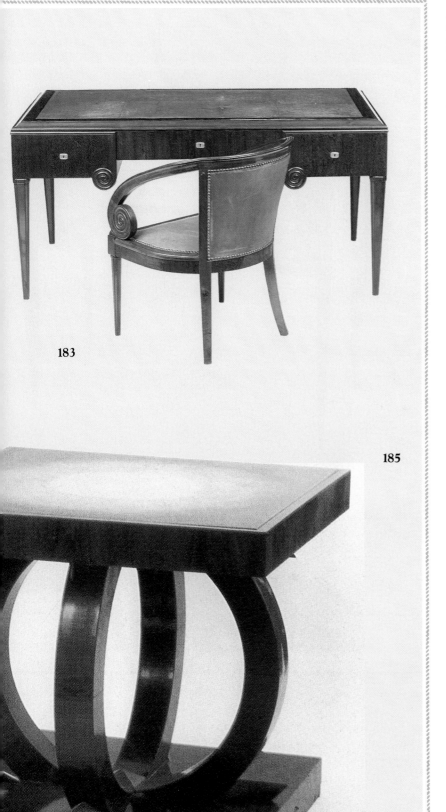

183

185

184. A Reproduction Table by Jacques-Henri Lartigue, originally designed c1918

This is a remake of the classic table by Lartigue (1894–1986), which was originally made of ivory and black-lacquered wood in 1918, and is now reproduced by the French designer/manufacturer Ecart.

Lartigue was known for his writing and photography as well as his furniture design, and he is associated with the Modern movement, which stressed function and utility as opposed to the sumptuous and luxurious excess of the Art Deco style. Le Corbusier's phrase, 'that houses are machines for living in', came to epitomize such ideals.

Here, Lartigue combines geometric shapes and exotic materials, which belong to the Art Deco repertoire, with the Modernist notion of structural simplicity. The bold, original, sculptural result feels quite at home in the 1980s.

185. A French Art Deco Ebony Side Table by Pierre Legrain, c1923

This table is undeniably from the Art Deco period, with its straight lines and smooth surfaces, and is made of an exotic wood with distinctive grain. Two influences of this era are in evidence here: the geometric shapes that were so popular give the table great elegance, and its form is directly taken from primitive art, which so fascinated French designers and artists at the start of the 20th century.

Pierre Legrain (1889–1929) was a furniture maker who pioneered this interest in the exotic – one of his most famous pieces is a low stool based on African designs and known as the *siège curule*. His designs were often made of luxurious materials, particularly lacquer, but also including mother-of-pearl and vellum. He lacked formal training as a cabinetmaker (which perhaps aided his innovative style), but found great success, working in the studio of Paul Iribe until 1914, then opening his own workshop in 1926.

186. The End Table by Gerrit Rietveld, originally designed c1923

Gerrit Rietveld (1888–1964) originally designed this table in 1923; this replica is made by the same cabinetmaker, G A van de Groenekan, who worked with Rietveld throughout his life on some of his most ambitious and bizarre compositions. The table was designed for the Schroeder house in Utrecht, and, like most of Rietveld's furniture, it was intended as part of an overall scheme based on basic architectural principles.

Apprenticed in the family firm, Rietveld set up his own workshop before training as an architect. Much of his early design was influenced by the principles of Dutch De Stijl (The Style) movement, which reduced objects to simple geometrical and linear elements and used the primary colours of red, blue and yellow as a contrast to the non-colours of black, white and grey. This table (and the Schroeder house generally) is a three-dimensional version of De Stijl ideas.

Rietveld's best-known work is the Red-Blue Chair, using the colours popularized by Piet Mondrian (1872–1944), who was most famous for his paintings of squares of colours. In retrospect, Rietveld could be considered the most revolutionary furniture maker of the early 20th century – he was certainly the earliest to produce radical new designs during and after the First World War.

187. The Berlin Chair by Gerrit Rietveld, c1923

This chair was created for the Berlin Exhibition of 1923. Like his End Table of the same date, the chair abandons all traditional preconceptions of symmetry and colour. In 1924, it was added to the Schroeder house in Utrecht, forming an unusual partnership with Rietveld's End Table.

189

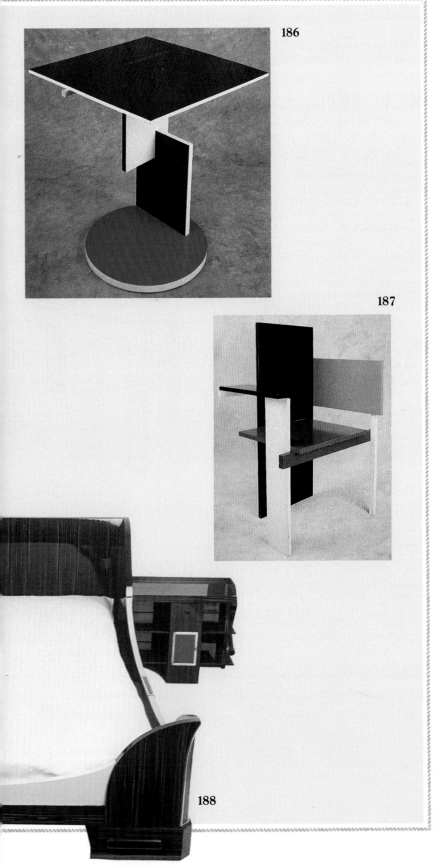

186

187

188

188. A French Art Deco Ebony Bed and Bedside Tables by Marcel Coard, *c*1925

The Art Deco movement reached its height during the 1920s, and was perhaps best known for its chairs, tables and interior designs. Marcel Coard (1889–1975) began designing furniture while recuperating from injuries sustained in the First World War. Afterward, he opened his own shop in Paris, first offering reproductions of period pieces, but soon creating Art Deco works for prominent clients.

Coard's most notable work was for Jacques Doucet's villa at Neuilly, outside Paris, designed by Pierre Legrain (1889–1929). Doucet, a couturier renowned for his collection of Old Master paintings 18th-century French antiques, sold this collection in 1912 and from then on concentrated on works by contemporary designers such as Coard, Paul Iribe and Eileen Gray, and painters such as Picasso, Modigliani and Henri Rousseau.

It is unusual to find a matching bed and bedside tables such as these, and especially ones so luxurious. The blue panels in the tables are lapis lazuli, surrounded by silver frames, and the wood is Macassar ebony. Elegantly simple, straight lines dominate but for the outward curve at the foot of the bed.

189. A French Art Deco Dressing Table by Emile-Jacques Ruhlmann, *c*1925

The furniture of Emile-Jacques Ruhlmann (1879-1933) is often compared to the work of the great 18th-century French cabinetmakers. Of excellent quality and made at great expense, pieces such as this table come from the peak of Ruhlmann's neo-classical phase. It is high Parisian Art Deco, with tapering legs, the use of exotic hardwoods (in this case, ebony), ivory details and panels in shagreen (sharkskin). The brass-capped *sabots* (literally, 'clogs') seen here were a particular trademark of his, echoing the mounts on 18th-century neo-classical furniture.

Ruhlmann wrote that it was 'the elite which launches fashion and determines its direction', and, not surprisingly, he was supported through much of his working life by wealthy patrons. He stated that the proportions of his furniture as a whole were far more important than their detail or ornament, but the luxury and style of his work – and especially his applied decoration – are outstanding.

190. A French Art Deco Bronze and Marble Table by Armand-Albert Rateau, c1925

Armand-Albert Rateau (1882–1938) was one of the most celebrated and eccentric metalworkers in Art Deco Paris; he was also a renowned interior decorator, and his extravagant designs for the apartment of the *couturière*, Jeanne Lanvin, were much admired.

His tables in particular were strikingly original. This example in bronze has a marble top in the form of a large tray, reminiscent of ancient Chinese ceremonial vessels. Its legs are the stylized forms of a bird, perhaps a peacock, and they have an archaic feel to them; indeed Rateau was directly influenced by the classical Roman furniture in metal he viewed on a visit to Herculaneum and Pompeii.

191. The Laccio Table by Marcel Breuer, c1925

Marcel Breuer (1902–1981) produced a design which became a near cliché of modern furniture – essentially comprising a chrome frame with leather stretched on it. The Wassily chair, also illustrated here, was made at the Bauhaus for Wassily Kandinsky's studio, and was the most celebrated example of this style; it has become a modern classic. This table originates from the same spirit.

Breuer was one of the most distinctive architects of the Modernist movement and designed extensively in Germany and the United States, where he also taught at Harvard. His interest lies in both structure and aesthetics, as can be seen from these early designs. The table is elegant and striking, with its combination of glass and chrome. These designs remain very popular, and although often associated with the 1960s, they date in fact to a time before even the motor car was popular.

192. A French Art Deco *Guéridon* by Jean Dunand, c1925

This table is clearly based on the traditional French two-tiered circular table form from the 18th century. Jean Dunand (1877–1942) was a radical designer from the Art Deco era, and specialized in lacquer work. The interest in lacquer in the 1920s stemmed from a search for the exotic (seen in the use of materials such as ebony and shagreen), and Dunand experimented by adding gold and silver dust, mother-of-pearl, ivory, etc, to his lacquers in the traditional Japanese style. He often worked for other designers, including Emile-Jacques Ruhlmann, on projects ranging in scale from jewellery to the interior of the

Smoking Room of the *Ambassade Française*, part of the *Paris Exposition des Arts Décoratifs et Industriels Modernes* in 1925.

Dunand's tables and chairs tend to have basic geometric shapes, with an emphasis on decoration rather than form.

193. A French Art Deco Two-tier Low Table by Louis Sognot, c1925

This stylish Art Deco table is veneered in palissander wood, an exotic variation of rosewood. Louis Sognot (1892–1970) was known for this combination of exotic woods with a metallic frame. An influential designer in France in the 1920s, he worked with the designer, Charlotte Alix, and the Primavera atelier, before exhibiting in Paris under his own name after 1923. Other unusual commissions of his included decorating the 1st-class Doctor's cabin on the famous 1920s ocean liner, *Normandie*, and working on interiors of the liner, *Atlantique*. He also lectured at the Ecole Boulle, a school of metalwork in Paris named after the 17th-century craftsman, André-Charles Boulle.

194. A Sharkskin and Ebony Table, c1930

Although unsigned, this table is probably by Clément Rousseau and bears a striking resemblance to a chair made by him in 1921. Rousseau was largely responsible for the revival of the use of shagreen (sharkskin), which he tinted in a variety of colours, usually green, and combined with exotic woods. He was also patronized by Jacques Doucet, and several of his pieces can be found in Doucet's villa at Neuilly.

Made of green-tinted sharkskin and ebony, the top of this table shows the sunburst motif widely used in the Art Deco era and a favourite of Rousseau's. This is very similar to the chair of 1921, which is made of a combination of sharkskin and walnut, and also bears the sunburst motif on the back. The table is heavier than the chair, however, and probably from about a decade later.

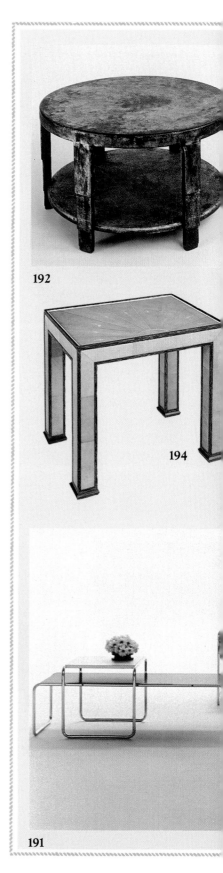

192

194

191

190

193

195. A Folding Writing Table by Paul Dupré-Lafon, c1930

This chic bureau was made for the family Lecroard and folds away to what must be the slimmest of desks. Supported on slender, square-sectioned shafts, a gilded leather flap folds down to form a working surface.

Little is known about Paul Dupré-Lafon (1900–1971), whose furniture in the main is unsigned. Like many Art Deco designers, he specialized in exotic materials, and his work is always of excellent quality, resulting in slim and elegant straight-edged shapes.

196. A Scandinavian Plywood Table by Alvar Aalto, c1931

The development of the simple, uncluttered wooden furniture that is today associated with Scandinavia, and especially Finland, was largely due to the work of Alvar Aalto (1898–1976). This talented and prodigious architect/designer was responsible for over 200 buildings, concerning himself with lighting, heating, acoustics and exterior surroundings as well as the basic design and construction. He saw furniture as an accessory to architecture, and believed that the human form should touch only natural materials. Wood is good acoustically as it absorbs sound, and Aalto's belief that it was pliable enough not to be cut or carved led to the development of his bent laminated plywood pieces.

One of Aalto's major projects was the Paimio Sanatorium in Finland, which he designed in the early 1930s. Much of the furniture for the hospital came from experimental design work he carried out with his wife, Aino Marsio, including this table and laminated bentwood chairs sometimes covered with a birch veneer.

197. An Oak Pineapple Coffee Table by Jean-Michel Frank, c1932

Jean-Michel Frank (1895–1941) was known for working with unusual materials and techniques. He used ordinary materials such as iron, straw and oak in luxurious pieces, often treating oak with lead to accentuate its patterned grain. Frank worked extensively with Adolphe Chanaux in the late 1920s; Chanaux had earlier worked with André Groult and Emile-Jacques Ruhlmann, leading figures of the Art Deco movement.

This table shows a typical 1930s combination of simplicity, in the flat planes of the surface, and substance, in the monumental legs. The legs are very thick compared to the elegant top, and decorated with a massive overlapping scale motif. As its title suggests, the table's decoration is taken from nature, although, like much decoration of the time, it is stylized beyond recognition.

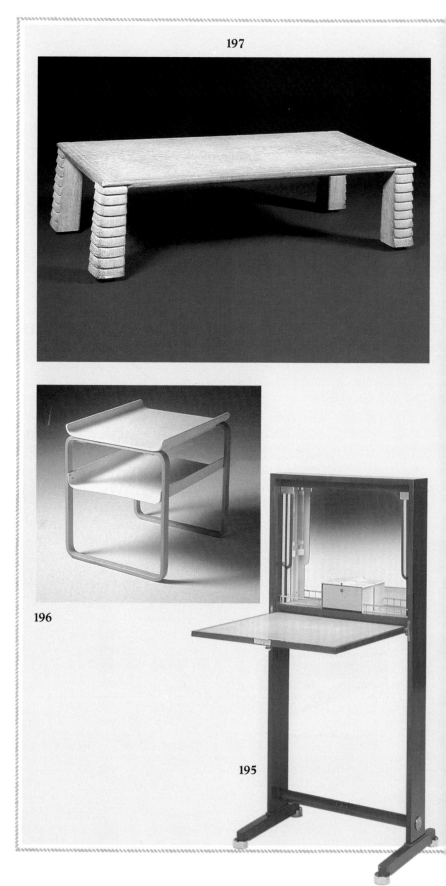

197

196

195

199

198

198. A French Fan Table by Pierre Chareau, c1933

This unusual, almost brutal, table has two fan-shaped rotating surfaces. The original design by Chareau (1883–1950) has been revived by the French furniture-making firm Ecart and is still manufactured today in Paris. Chareau was active at the 1925 Paris Exposition, and divided his time between building and furniture design: his *Maison de Verre* (House of Glass), completed in 1931, was the first to use glass tiles on the house's exterior, which later became a 1930s hallmark. Chareau's furniture was usually designed for the inside of his own commissions and was often made of highly polished woods.

Here, however, the patinated wrought iron used is simply waxed; thus it retains its industrial, utilitarian character. Although French, the table manifests a Bauhaus-like emphasis on utility.

199. A Pair of Bedside Tables by Paul Dupré-Lafon, c1935

These bedside tables were made for the villa, Les Myrtes, near Ste. Maxime, France. At this time, the South of France was the winter home for many of the rich and famous, including Noël Coward and Jean Cocteau, and other clients of Dupré-Lafon's included the Rothschild and Dreyfus families.

In keeping with his fascination with exotic materials, these bedside tables are covered in parchment, made out of finely stretched animal skin, and traditionally used for writing. The drawer fronts are covered in leather by the exclusive Hermès company – with which Dupré-Lafon worked repeatedly – and the tables sit on bases of black marble.

113

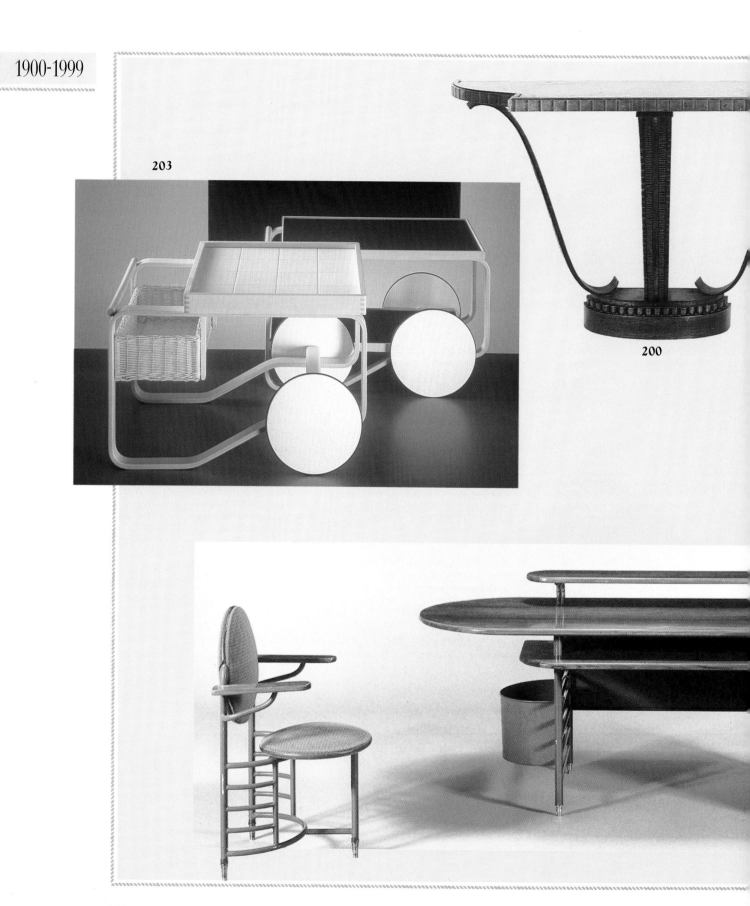

203

200

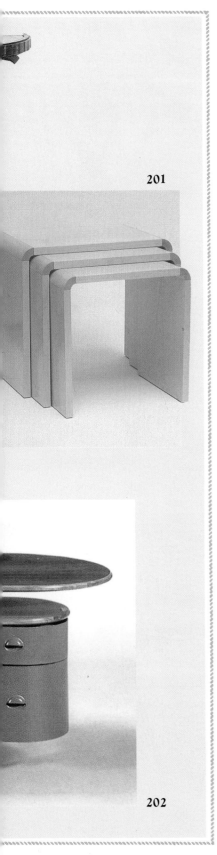

201

202

200. A French Wrought-iron Console Table by Raymond Subes, *c*1935

This breakfront table with black marble top (its centre section set slightly forward) echoes Georgian bookcases of the 18th century. The designers of the Art Deco era, especially Ruhlmann, used many neo-classical features in their designs.

Raymond Subes (1893–1970), born in Paris, studied metal engraving at the Parisian school of metalwork, the Ecole Boulle, before working with the influential architects, Borderel and Robert. In 1919 he became the director of their metal atelier, and was responsible for many influential architectural projects. He usually worked in wrought iron, but also used bronze, copper and aluminium.

Sube's work followed on from that of Emile Robert, who was responsible for the revival of metalwork as an Arts & Crafts interest in the 19th century, and the great Art Deco metalworker, Edgar Brandt (1880–1960). Brandt and Subes both worked for the top designers of the time and exhibited under their own names.

201. French *Tables Gigogne* by Frank and Chanaux, *c*1935

Gigogne is the French word for a mother of many children. These tables were originally created in oak and covered in vellum and straw marquetry. The partnership of Jean-Michel Frank (1895–1941) and Adolphe Chanaux (1887–1965) produced some original work from their design studios in Paris.

In 1927, Frank commissioned Chanaux to decorate his apartment to his own design and so began a professional association that ended only with Frank's suicide in New York, shortly after the outbreak of World War II. The two sometimes collaborated with their immediate neighbours, including Salvador Dali, Alberto and Diego Giacometti, and Pablo Picasso, and among their well-known patrons were Mr and Mrs Nelson Rockefeller, Elsa Schiaparelli and Templeton Crocker of San Francisco.

Frank/Chanaux furniture was known for its sparseness and simplicity of line and function; on visiting Frank's apartment, Jean Cocteau remarked that Frank was a nice young man, but it was a pity the burglars took everything.

202. An American Writing Table and Chair by Frank Lloyd Wright, *c*1936

This range of furniture, Cherokee Red, was made from enamelled steel and American walnut. It was designed by Frank Lloyd Wright (1867–1959), the most famous American 20th-century architect, for the Johnson Wax Building in Racine, Wisconsin. Wright's body of work covered many periods, from Victorian styles up to 20th-century post-war designs, and his furniture reflected many of these eras, in the main because they were designed for actual interiors. Wright felt that architecture and furniture were an integral whole, and he occasionally made pieces in the same shape as the buildings they were placed in. He was much influenced by Charles Rennie Mackintosh and was as equally innovative.

Wright favoured long, low shapes, as seen in his 'prairie houses' in architecture, designed to harmonize with the prairies in which they were set. The writing table featured concentrates on the horizontal; the desk and chair come from Wright's utilitarian era, and reflect his interest in unornamented design.

203. A Tea Trolley by Alvar Aalto, *c*1937

Alvar Aalto (1898–1976) was a leading architect of Modernism, a movement closely associated with the German Bauhaus. This tea trolley was exhibited at the Paris World's Fair of 1937, and is a 20th-century descendant of serving tables, sometimes mobile, which had been produced since the 17th century. The original form was the 'dumb waiter', a three-tiered table on castors which could be placed or wheeled near to the main dining table 'as soon as supper is over' so that 'our conversation was not under any restraint by servants in ye room' (Mrs Hamilton's Diary, 1874).

This trolley shows a typical freshness of design and lack of decoration; it is at once attractive and functional. Aalto founded the firm Artek in 1935, a plywood manufacturer still in operation today.

204. An Italian Card Table by Carlo Graffi, c1950

The influence of the Milan school, particularly its premier exponent, Carlo Mollino, is clear in Graffi's juxtaposition of materials – in this case, wood and glass – on this card table. The wood is unconventionally cut into a shape which is not inherently strong but is stressed by tensioning bars, a technique used extensively by Mollino in the 1940s and 1950s. There are also similarities to 18th-century neo-classical card tables: it is stylish, with straight legs and severe outlines, and trays for the counters slide out from each of the corners, just as candlestick holders slid out from beneath such tables in the 1700s.

Although the Milan school was responsible for countless innovative ideas, many have not endured very well. This table, with its conflicting angles and clashing horizontal and vertical lines, is energetic, but not restful.

205. Pedestal Tables by Eero Saarinen, c1955

Tables supported by a single pedestal reached their peak of popularity in the early 19th century; however, the weakness of design of the wooden joint generally led to stocky pedestals. Here, Saarinen uses modern materials to produce a more elegant range of chairs and tables. The Pedestal range was first produced in the early 1950s and has been manufactured ever since – one set is permanently on display in New York's Museum of Modern Art.

Finnish-born Eero Saarinen (1910–61) was the son of the famous architect, Eliel Saarinen. After studying sculpture in Paris, he graduated from the Yale School of Architecture. Despite the fact that he is basically American, his furniture shows much Scandinavian elegance and desire for simplicity. He once declared that 'the underside of typical chairs and tables makes a confusing, unrestful world. I want to clear up the slum of legs.'

206. An Italian Desk with Formica Top by Carlo Mollino, c1955

This pedestal desk is a curious combination of blond wood and Formica. It is typical of Mollino's post-Second World War work, when his designs were sculptural and often humorous. This table, for example, is not purely functional – the pedestal, placed on one side, could have been under the desk top, and the stretchers could have been simpler. The leg construction of this table seems to resemble a bat, or an aeroplane.

Italian design received considerable impetus after the Second World War, when so

much that had been destroyed needed to be replaced economically. Designers and artists in the post-war period were keen to use new materials such as Formica, and many of Mollino's earlier designs used the cheaper plywood. His later work, such as this, echoes the stressed plywood construction of his chairs, although here he is using solid cut timber for the framework.

Mollino (1905–73) was a prominent member of the Milan school of design, which initially gained attention at the first Milan Triennale Exhibition of 1933, a fair which continues to today. His work has often been associated with Franco Albini and Guiseppe Terragni, the architects, and much of his furniture was produced by Appelli of Turin.

207. A Trapezoidal Harpies Coffee Table by Alberto Giacometti, c1955

This table comes from a series of bronze and glass furniture based on skeletal human and organic forms. Here, the form of a harpy – a mythical monster with a woman's head and body and limbs of a bird – is used as decoration on the twig-like legs and stretcher. The whole piece is cast in bronze.

Giacometti (1901–66) was a Swiss-born sculptor/painter/poet who trained in Italy in the 1920s; while there, he was much influenced by the Rumanian-born sculptor, Constantin Brancusi (1876-1957). In the 1930s, Giacometti produced mainly surreal work with mythological and mysterious elements, and later went on to concentrate on stick-like emaciated figures, made from a wire frame applied with plaster of Paris. His furniture is generally fairly light-hearted, and is very much prized by collectors of 20th-century work.

208. The Green Table by Allen Jones, c1972

This table is by the Pop Art sculptor, Allen Jones, (b.1937) and is one of a limited edition of six made of glass fibre, leather and other accessories. It is provocatively sexual, although less so than his former series, *Table Sculpture,* which featured semi-naked women wearing only gloves and boots. This has little place in the history of functional furniture, but it carries on the precedent of fantasy furniture as seen in 18th-century Rococo work, earlier Baroque pieces and the designs of the 20th-century Surrealist, Salvador Dali, who in 1936 designed a sofa after Mae West's lips. This table is a curious twist to the traditional use of human figures to support tables and other furniture, a device common in the late 17th century and early 18th century.

206

205

204

208

207

1900-1999

209. A Low Table Designed by Andrée Putman, c1978

This low table is clearly influenced by designers such as Jacques-Henri Lartigue, with its strong flavour of Art Deco revival – straight lines, flat surfaces and pyramidal, many-sided legs which give it a sculptural quality occupying space. The top has a low apron around it which gives the whole piece an impression of solidity. The table's feeling of monumentality is reminscent of early Art Deco designers, and the black-lacquered wood it comprises was a typical Art Deco medium.

Andrée Putman is a Parisian interior designer, many of whose furniture creations have been produced by Ecart International.

210. The Zig Zag Table by Jeremy Broun, c1979

Contemporary furniture production falls into three general categories – mass productions for economy; commercial designer furniture; and limited-edition designer furniture. This last provides the closest link between the maker and user, and often results in the most interesting products. This can be clearly seen in the creations of the successful craft revival begun in the 1960s.

This table is made from hyedua – an oriental hardwood – by Bath cabinetmaker and designer Jeremy Boun (b.1945). It exploits the markings of traditional manufacture, as seen by the wood joints where the top meets the legs, and is innovative in its centre joint in the table top. It is based on traditional craft design, as opposed to radical modern design; tables based on the principle of three have been made since the 16th century, but the triangular component has more usually been the tripod base rather than the top, as here.

211. The Spyder Table by Ettore Sottsass, c1980
and
212. The Shift Table by Ettore Sottsass, c1980

The 1980s revival of interest in structure was an extension of ideas from Breuer and the Bauhaus of the 1920s, although most of the later pieces employ a more sophisticated combination of colour and engineering, as here, to form the central support.

Sottsass was born in 1917 in Austria, and has worked with bodies as diverse as Olivetti and the Royal College of Art, promoting the radical Memphis Collection in Milan. Describing himself as 'a metaphoric designer', he considers the object itself to be relatively unimportant; rather, he is more concerned with how it is presented. This he achieves by

using bright colours and unusual shapes. His furniture is said to show a sense of irony and wit, and often refers to human or animal form – the Spyder table, for instance, is appropriately named.

The Shift Table similarly appeals for its wit; it gives the impression that it is about to collapse. Its legs are in fact pinned together, and the visible parts rest on an inner iron structure. This table is also made in marble, resembling the classical columns of antiquity.

213. The Mega Table by Enrico Baleri, 1982

The broad, flat planes of this table are without colour or ornamentation, giving it a monumental feel that seems to refer to Classical ideas. The only decorative elements, apart from the table-top texture, are the vertical lines on the legs, which are reminiscent of fluting on classical columns. This is classicism taken to an extreme, 'abstracting' some of the aspects of ancient Roman architecture.

Baleri's work was produced by Knoll International, an American firm which specializes in reproducing 20th-century classics and which also produces Ettore Sottsass's work. The interest shown here in mass and form has been central to the work of a group of 1980s designers, who also include Vico Magistretti and Giandomenico Belotti.

214. Solomon's Table by Danny Lane, c1988

Is this a table or a piece of sculpture? Perhaps both. Made of marble and glass, it resembles a surfboard or fish suspended by towering piles of cut glass. Glass constructions such as this have become the trademark of Danny Lane (b.1955), an Illinois native who now lives in London and ranks among the most successful of 1980s designers. Lane claims that his pieces evolve naturally out of the medium he is using.

This bold design utilizes light and colour to show the materials to good effect; very much the same principles, in fact, that designers of all periods, whether Baroque, Rococo, Regency, Federal or Bauhaus, have employed in furniture making over the centuries.

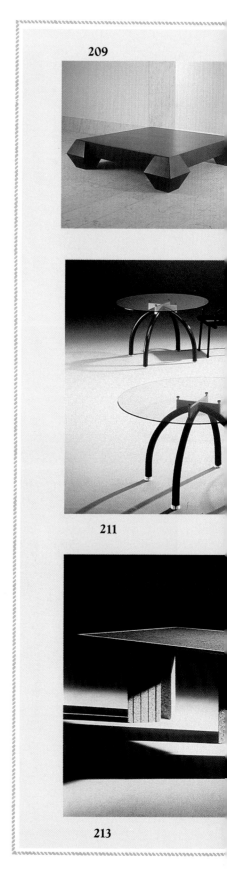

209

211

213

210

212

214

Monarchs

The names of English and French monarchs are often used to denote the period of a piece of furniture when the precise date of manufacture is not known.

In some cases a ruler is closely associated with a recognisable style; Louis XIV, for instance, saw the development of the decorative arts in France as a matter of policy and the massive formal designs of his time reflect the elaboration of life at his court. Dramatic upheavals such as the French Revolution brought about dramatic changes in style but generally changes of style were gradual and overlapped the reigns of different monarchs.

In Britain especially, the machinery of fashion tended to be more loosely linked to the sovereign and public taste was influenced by a variety of factors. This was especially true during the reign of long-lived monarchs like George III (1760-1820) and the names of the producers of cabinetmakers' pattern books, like Chippendale, Sheraton and Hepplewhite are often used quite freely to denote the style of their times. These cabinetmakers were influential not necessarily because of their designs but because they recorded contemporary styles, some of which of course may have been their own.

American furniture periods tend to be classified using a mixture of English monarchs and makers, and the dating is complicated by the fact that it took a long time for European styles to cross the Atlantic so that the American period occurs several years behind the corresponding period in Britain. For example, Queen Anne died in 1714, but the American Queen Anne style is taken to cover the period 1720-1750.

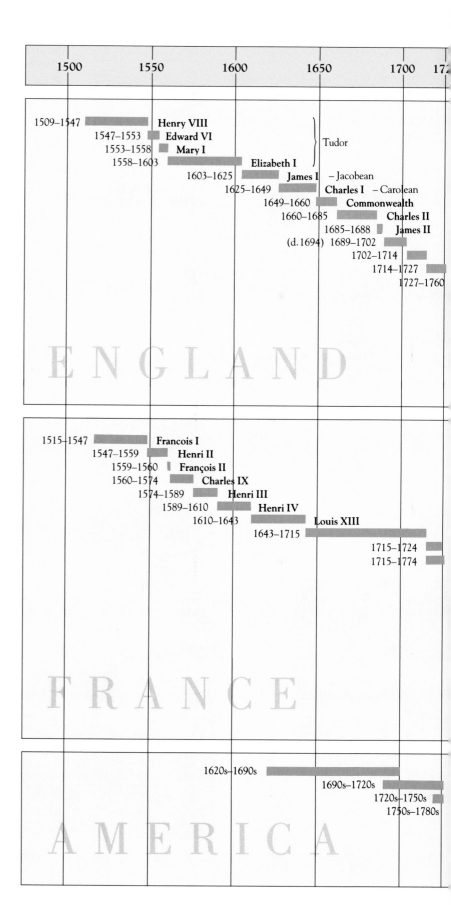

120

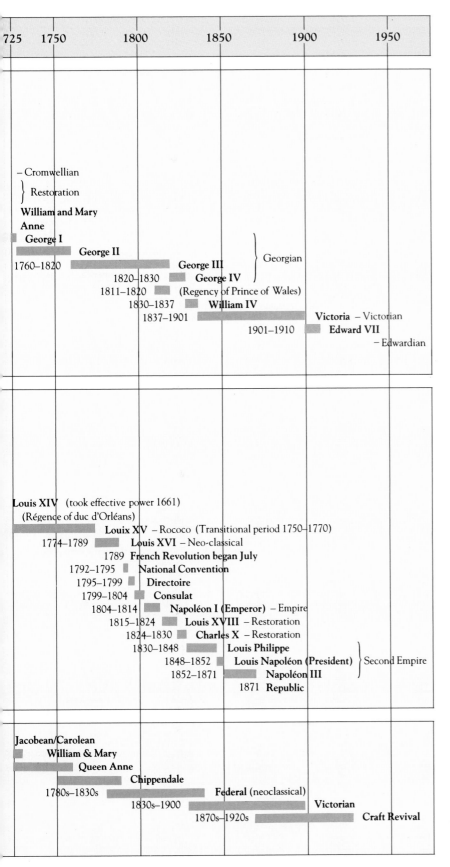

725	1750	1800	1850	1900	1950

– Cromwellian

} Restoration

William and Mary

Anne

George I

1760–1820   **George II**

      1820–1830   **George III** } Georgian

      1811–1820   **George IV**

      1830–1837   (Regency of Prince of Wales)

      1837–1901   **William IV**

        1901–1910   **Victoria** – Victorian

         Edward VII

         – Edwardian

Louis XIV (took effective power 1661)

(Régence of duc d'Orléans)

   Louix XV – Rococo (Transitional period 1750–1770)

1774–1789   **Louis XVI** – Neo-classical

    1789   **French Revolution began July**

1792–1795   **National Convention**

1795–1799   **Directoire**

1799–1804   **Consulat**

  1804–1814   **Napoléon I (Emperor)** – Empire

   1815–1824   **Louis XVIII** – Restoration

   1824–1830   **Charles X** – Restoration

   1830–1848   **Louis Philippe**

     1848–1852   **Louis Napoléon (President)** } Second Empire

     1852–1871   **Napoléon III**

      1871   **Republic**

Jacobean/Carolean

   William & Mary

     Queen Anne

      Chippendale

1780s–1830s   **Federal** (neoclassical)

   1830s–1900   **Victorian**

    1870s–1920s   **Craft Revival**

Cabinetmakers' pattern books and other influential publications

Listed here is a selection of books influential both on the furniture makers and designers of their times and on furniture historians.

Stalker and Parker, **Treatise of Japanning and Varnishing**, 1688

Thomas Chippendale, **Gentleman and Cabinet-Maker's Director**, 1754 (2nd edition 1755; 3rd edition 1762)

Ince and Mayhew, **Universal System of Household Furniture**, 1759–1762

Robert Manwaring, **Cabinet and Chair-Maker's Real Friend and Companion** 1765

Robert and James Adam, **Works in Architecture**, 1773–1778 (2nd volume 1779; 3rd volume 1822)

George Hepplewhite, **Cabinet-Maker and Upholsterer's Guide**, 1788

Thomas Shearer, Hepplewhite and others, **Cabinet-Maker's London Book of Prices**, 1788

Thomas Sheraton, **Cabinet-Maker and Upholsterer's Drawing-Book**, 1791–1794

Percier and Fontaine, **Receuil des décorations intérieurs**, 1801 (2nd edition 1812)

Thomas Sheraton, **Cabinet Dictionary**, 1803

Thomas Hope, **Household Furniture and Interior Decoration**, 1807

George Smith, **Collection of Designs for Household Furniture and Interior Decoration**, 1808

   Collection of Ornamental Designs after the Antique, 1812

   Cabinet Maker and Upholsterer's Guide, 1826

John C. Loudon, **Encyclopaedia of Cottage, Farm and Villa Furniture**, 1833

Augustus W.N. Pugin, **Gothic Furniture in the style of the 15th century**, 1835

   The True Principle of Pointed or Christian Architecture, 1841

Bruce Talbert, **Gothic Forms Applied to Furniture**, 1867

Charles Eastlake, **Hints on Household Taste**, 1868

121

acanthus – A Classical ornamental device based on the prickly, indented leaves of the acanthus plant, used especially in the capitals of Corinthian and Composite columns.

anthemion – A Classical ornament consisting of a band of alternating floral forms based on the honeysuckle flower. A single motif based on the honeysuckle is also called an anthemion.

apron – An ornamental projection below a rail, often shaped and carved.

arcading – A series of round-topped arches, frequently used decoratively, especially on early carved furniture.

astragal – A small half-round moulding frequently used for glazing bars.

ball and claw foot – A foot in the form of a claw clutching a ball, often used in conjunction with a cabriole leg and popular in England and America in the 18th century.

baluster–turned – See turned leg.

banding – Veneer was often used in bands to form decorative borders to the main surface. Crossbanding was cut across the grain, while feather or herringbone banding was cut with the grain at an angle so that two strips laid side by side resembled a feather.

barleysugar-turned – See turned leg.

Baroque – A decorative style which originated in Italy and reached its height in the 17th century, characterized by heavy and exuberant forms. Its influence varied from country to country but Baroque furniture tends to be sculptural and often architectural in form and is frequently gilded, with human figures, scrolls and shells much in evidence.

beading – A three-dimensional decorative motif in the form of a series of round beads in a single line or a very fine half-round moulding (see cock beading).

Biedermeier – A German term used to denote both the period 1815–1848 and the decorative style popular in Germany, Austria and Scandinavia from the 1820s to the 1840s, which was characterized by solid, unpretentious furniture in light-coloured woods. Biedermeier was a newspaper caricature symbolising the uncultured bourgeois.

bobbin-turned – See turned leg.

bombé – An exaggeratedly curved and swollen form characteristic of the Rococo style.

boulle – A distinctive form of marquetry decoration making use of metal and other veneers, usually brass and tortoiseshell, to form a rich pattern. It takes its name from André-Charles Boulle, *ébéniste* to Louis XIV, who perfected but did not invent a technique known in Italy since the late 17th century. The method of production, cutting the design from layers of brass and tortoiseshell glued together, resulted in two sets of veneer. One has the pattern in brass against tortoiseshell (known as *première partie*), the second is the other way round (*contre-partie*).

breakfast table – A snap top table where the top tilts vertically on the pedestal for storage, usually after breakfast is cleared. 'Snap' refers to the sound made by the catch (which is like a yale lock) when the table is tilted down for use.

breakfront – A term used to describe a piece of furniture where one or more sections project from the main body of the piece.

brown furniture – A term used by the antiques trade to refer to the plain English mahogany furniture of the Georgian period.

bulb-turned – See turned leg.

bureau – The French word for all kinds of writing desks, often further defined, as in bureau plat or bureau à cylindre. The word is derived from *bure*, a coarse cloth used to cover the writing tables of clerks and secretaries in the Middle Ages. In Britain bureau has come to mean a slope-front writing desk of traditional pattern; but in America it is used to describe a dressing chest, often with a mirror.

burl – The American term for burr.

burr – See veneer.

C-scroll – A scroll in the shape of a letter C, a favourite Rococo motif.

cabochon – An oval or round boss used decoratively, usually in conjunction with other motifs.

cabriole leg – A sinuous tapering leg, curving outwards at the knee, in towards the ankle and out again at the foot.

canted – When legs or projected members are set at an angle to the corner of a piece they are known as canted legs or canted corners.

capital – The head of a column, usually decorated according to the different architectural orders, i.e. Doric (plain disc-like capital), Ionic (with four scroll corners), Corinthian (decorated with bands of acanthus leaves), Composite (a combination of Ionic and Corinthian).

cartouche – An ornamental panel, often a stylized shield, which is decorative itself but can also carry an inscription, a monogram or a crest.

caryatid – An architectural motif consisting of a column in the form of a male or female figure which is also often found on carved furniture and as a bronze mount.

castors – Small swivelling wheels attached to the bottom of furniture, to make it easier to move the piece.

chamfer – A narrow flat surface formed by cutting away the apex of an angle between two surfaces, thus removing the sharp edge. Hence chamfered leg, chamfered stretcher etc.

chasing – The tooling of a metal's surface. Bronze furniture mounts were chased after casting to remove blemishes and sharpen the detail before gilding.

chinoiserie – A Western imitation of Chinese decoration, usually more fanciful than accurate and frequently used to give an exotic touch to a basically European design.

ciseleur – French for a craftsman who used a variety of chisels and other tools to finish bronze mounts once they had been cast by a *fondeur* or founder. After finishing they were usually gilded by a *doreur*. Under the 18th century Paris guild system the *fondeurs-ciseleurs* and the *doreurs* had separate Corporations.

cock beading – A very fine half-round moulding applied around the edges of drawer-fronts.

contre-partie – see boulle.

cornice – An architectural term used in the description of furniture for the top moulding of bookcases and other large pieces, many of which were conceived along architectural lines.

cornucopia – A horn of plenty, used decoratively as a shell-like horn overflowing with fruit.

cresting – The carved ornament on the top rail of a chair-back.

cresting rail – See top rail.

crocket – A leaf-like projection frequently placed on angles, arches and pinnacles in Gothic architecture and found as a decorative device on Gothic style furniture.

crossbanding – See banding.

cut-card work – A form of slightly raised decoration mainly used on silverware, consisting of thin sheets cut into patterns and soldered onto the surface.

doreur – See ciseleur.

ébéniste – A French term for a cabinetmaker, a specialist in veneered furniture, as distinct from a *menuisier* or joiner who specialized in carved pieces like chairs or beds. A *maître* of the Paris furniture makers' guild (*Corporation des menuisiers-ébénistes*) was not bound to specialize, but the distinction was generally observed until the end of the 18th century.

escutcheon – A plate surrounding and protecting a keyhole.

espagnolette – A decorative motif in the form of a female head surrounded by a stylized lace ruff, much favoured as mounts during the Régence period.

estampille – The stamp with the name and initials of a *maître ébéniste* which was obligatory on French furniture from about 1750 until the Revolution. The mark was struck with a cold punch rather than branded, although delicate pieces could be signed in ink. Long names were sometimes shortened, as in BVRB for Bernard van Risenburgh, and the marks were usually in an inconspicuous place, often accompanied by the monogram of the *Corporation des Jurés Menuisiers-Ebénistes* – JME conjoined – a quality control mark. Furniture made for the crown did not have to be stamped and royal craftsmen were exempt.

festoon – A neo-Classical decorative motif in the form of a looped garland of flowers, fruit and foliage.

figure – The natural grain patterns of a veneer are known as figuring.

finial – An ornamental projection from the top of a piece of furniture, often a knob, ball, acorn, urn or flame.

fluting – Decorative in the form of shallow, parallel grooves, especially on columns and pilasters or on the legs of furniture.

fondeur – See ciseleur.

fretwork – Carved geometrical patterns, either in relief or pierced, or sawn with a fretsaw.

frieze – An architectural term for the flat surface beneath a cornice, used loosely to describe flat horizontal members in furniture, especially below table tops and the cornices of case furniture.

gadroon – A form of decorative edging usually in the form of a series of convex curved lobes or repeated spiral ribs resembling ropetwist.

gallery – A miniature railing, often of brass, placed around the edge of a table or desk top to prevent papers and other small objects slipping off.

gilding – The application of gold to the surface of another material. Bronze mounts were frequently gilded to prevent tarnishing, especially in France.

Wood was also gilded for decorative effect.

gilt – See gilding.

Gothic – A decorative style based on the pointed arches, cluster columns, spires and other elements of late medieval architecture. Gothic revivals have influenced furniture design at several periods, particularly in Britain in the mid-18th century and again in the mid-19th century.

grisaille – Monochrome decoration in tones of grey.

inlay – Although it is often used to mean marquetry, inlay strictly refers to decorative materials like ivory or ebony set into the surface of solid wood, unlike veneer which covers the whole surface.

japanning – The term used in America and Britain for techniques imitating the Oriental lacquerwork which began to arrive in Europe via the Dutch East India Company in the 17th century.

joinery – Joined furniture is formed of vertical and horizontal members, united by mortice and tenon joints and supporting panels.

lowboy – A late 17th or 18th century American dressing table on legs, sometimes found combined with a slope-front desk.

maître – A master craftsman under the Paris guild system, who was entitled to own a workshop and stamp his pieces, having served an apprenticeship and paid the necessary fees. See *estampille*.

marchand-mercier – Under the Paris guild system *marchands- merciers* combined the roles of furniture dealers and interior decorators. They were not allowed to run their own workshops but often exerted considerable influence on fashion by acting as intermediaries between customer and craftsman.

marquetry – The use of veneers (woods of different colours, bone, ivory, mother-of-pearl, tortoiseshell, etc.) to form decorative designs like scrolls, flowers and landscapes. Abstract geometrical patterns formed in the same manner are known as parquetry.

member – Any of the structural components (rails, uprights, stretchers etc.) of a piece of joined furniture.

menuisier – See *ébéniste*.

mortice and tenon joint – The basic method of joining the framework of a piece of furniture. The tenon is a projection (usually a slim rectangle) at the end of a rail which fits exactly into the mortice, a cavity cut in the side of an upright. The tenon is normally secured by dowels.

moulding – A length of wood or other material applied to the surface of a piece of furniture. The shaped section of a moulding is usually made up from a number of curves, and there are various standard types (astragal, ogee, cavetto, ovolo) mostly of architectural origin.

mounts – Decorative motifs, usually of brass or gilt-bronze, fixed to cabinetwork.

neo-Classicism – The predominant decorative style of the second half of the 18th century. Based on the restrained use of Greek and Roman architectural form and ornament, it is characterised by a sober, rectilinear emphasis which was a conscious reaction to the exuberance of the Rococo.

ormolu – Gilt bronze. A term derived from the French *or moulu* (literally ground gold).

panel – A flat surface supported by rails and stiles in joined furniture.

parcel gilt – Gilded in part only.

parquetry – See marquetry.

patera – A neo-Classical decorative motif, either oval or round, resembling a stylized flower or rosette.

pierced – Carved ornament is described as pierced when the decoration is cut right through the piece, as in fretwork.

pilaster – A shallow column attached to a piece of furniture.

première partie – see boulle.

putto (pl. putti) – A naked infant, often winged, used as a decorative motif. Also referred to as a cherub, a cupid or an amoretto.

rail – A horizontal member used in the construction of joined furniture.

reeding – Decoration in the form of parallel ribbing, especially on columns and pilasters or on the legs of furniture.

Renaissance – The rebirth of ancient Roman values in the arts which began in Italy in the 14th century and gradually replaced the Gothic style in most of Europe during the following two and a half centuries. Renaissance designers were inspired by the sculpture and architectural remains of the ancient world and their furniture reflects this in the profusion of carved ornament.

repoussé work – A form of embossed decoration produced by hammering sheet metal from the underside.

rocaille – Stylised and fanciful rock and shell decoration, used by extension to refer to many of the decorative forms of the Rococo.

Rococo – A decorative style which spread from France during the first half of the 18th century, characterised by delicate curved outlines, C-scrolls, fantastic organic forms and a tendency towards asymmetry in ornamental details.

sabre leg – A furniture leg which is curved and tapered like a cavalry sabre.

seat rail – The horizontal framework which supports the seat of a joined chair.

serpentine – In the form of an undulating curve, convex at the centre and concave on each side.

spindle – A slim, turned rod frequently used as an upright in chair backs.

splat – The central upright member of a chair back which joins the seat to the top rail.

square-section leg – A leg which would be square if cut at right- angles, but which may also be tapering or shaped in some other way.

stile – A vertical member used in the construction of joined furniture.

strapwork – A form of decoration particularly popular in Northern Europe in the 16th and 17th centuries, resembling interlaced, pierced and scrolled bands of leather.

stretcher – A horizontal crosspiece used to join and strengthen the legs of a piece of furniture.

stringing – Thin strips of wood or metal inlay used to decorate furniture.

strung border – A border decorated with stringing.

swag – A decorative motif in the form of a loop of cloth and similar to a festoon.

table en chiffonière – A small 18th century French work table witha high gallery around the top and several drawers in the frieze, often fitted with a writing drawer or slide.

timbers – Another name for the heavy wooden framework of a piece of furniture.

turned leg – A leg shaped on a lathe, usually circular in section and mainly fashionable before the beginning of the 18th century. Turned legs are found in many traditional patterns, e.g. bobbin – a series of small bulbs or bobbins; bobbin and ring – small bulbs interspaced by rings; bulb – a large bulbous swelling of elongated melon form, often carved and used with a base and capital to form a leg; barley-sugar or barley-twist – a double spiral resembling a barleysugar sweet; vase – in the shape of a vase, usually slim at the base and gradually increasing in diameter towards the top; baluster – in the shape of a baluster, bulbous at the base and slim towards the top.

under-frame – The supporting structure of a piece of furniture, including legs, stretchers and any other braces.

uprights – The vertical parts of a chair back, formed as continuations of the rear legs.

vase-turned – See turned leg.

veneer – A very thin sheet, usually of wood, applied to the surface of a piece of furniture. Veneers cut from knotty areas of the tree are particularly decorative and known as burrs, hence burr walnut, for example.

vernis Martin – A generic term for varnish and lacquer (japanning) used in France in imitation of oriental lacquer, but specifically referring to the four Martin brothers, who were granted a monopoly on imitation relief lacquer in 1730, which was renewed in 1744. Their speciality was painted furniture to which *vernis Martin* most often refers.

vitruvian scroll – A Classically-derived ornamental device in the form of a series of scrolls resembling waves.

woods – Although some woods are distinctive, the majority have so many species that it is hard to identify each separate type. Ebony, for example, comes in 90 different tree types, all of which have different grains and characteristics, such as hardness, colour, etc. Zebrawood, for example, closely resembles calamander (from Sri Lanka) and coromandel (from India), and can be difficult to distinguish from black rosewood and striped ebony.

x-frame – An arrangement of diagonal stretchers joining the front and back legs of a piece of furniture and crossing to form an X.

x-stretcher – See x-frame.

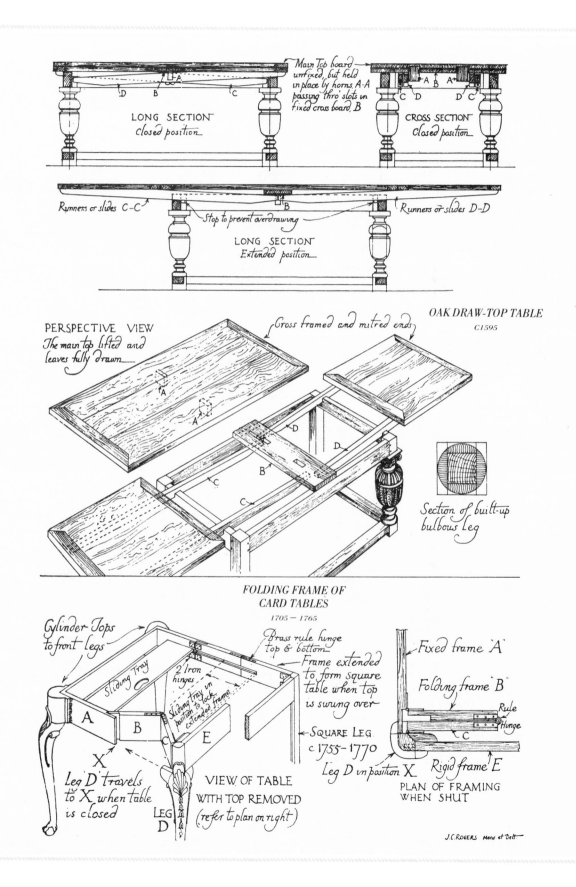

Main Top board unfixed, but held in place by horns A-A passing thro' slots in fixed cross board, B

LONG SECTION
Closed position

CROSS SECTION
Closed position

Runners or slides C-C

Stop to prevent overdrawing

Runners or slides D-D

LONG SECTION
Extended position

OAK DRAW-TOP TABLE
C1595

PERSPECTIVE VIEW
The main top lifted and leaves fully drawn

Cross framed and mitred ends

Section of built-up bulbous Leg

FOLDING FRAME OF
CARD TABLES
1705 — 1765

Cylinder Tops to front legs

Sliding Tray

2 Iron hinges

Brass rule hinge top & bottom

Frame extended to form square table when top is swung over

Sliding Tray in position to lock extended frame

Fixed frame "A"

Folding frame "B"

Rule Hinge

SQUARE LEG
c 1755–1770

Leg D in position X

Rigid frame "E"

Leg D travels to X when table is closed

LEG D

VIEW OF TABLE
WITH TOP REMOVED
(refer to plan on right)

PLAN OF FRAMING
WHEN SHUT

J.C.ROGERS Mens et Delt

124

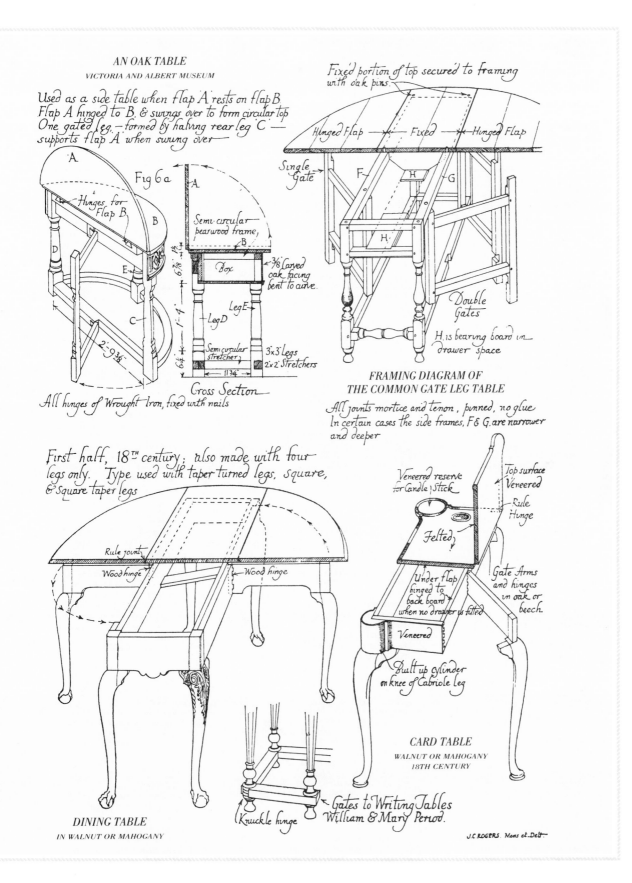

AN OAK TABLE
VICTORIA AND ALBERT MUSEUM

Used as a side table when flap A rests on flap B.
Flap A hinged to B. & swings over to form circular top
One gated leg. — formed by halving rear leg C —
supports flap A when swung over

Fig 6 a

Hinges for Flap B

A

B

D

E

Leg E

Leg D

C

2'·9⅜"

6·7"

1'·4"

6⅛"

Semi-circular pearwood frame,

Box

⅜ Carved oak facing bent to curve.

Semi-circular stretcher

3x3 Legs 2x2 Stretchers

11¾"

Cross Section

All hinges of Wrought Iron, fixed with nails

Fixed portion of top secured to framing with oak pins.

Hinged Flap — Fixed — Hinged Flap

Single Gate

F

H

G

H

Double Gates

H is bearing board in drawer space

FRAMING DIAGRAM OF THE COMMON GATE LEG TABLE

All joints mortice and tenon, pinned, no glue
In certain cases the side frames, F & G. are narrower and deeper

First half, 18ᵗʰ century; also made with four
legs only. Type used with taper turned legs, square,
& square taper legs

Rule joint
Wood hinge
Wood hinge

Veneered reserve for Candle Stick

Top surface Veneered

Rule Hinge

Felted

Under flap hinged to back board when no drawer is fitted

Veneered

Built up cylinder on knee of Cabriole leg

Gate Arms and hinges in oak or beech.

CARD TABLE
WALNUT OR MAHOGANY
18TH CENTURY

DINING TABLE
IN WALNUT OR MAHOGANY

Knuckle hinge

Gates to Writing Tables
William & Mary Period.

J.C. ROGERS. Mens et Delt

DATE DUE